11+ Non-verbal Reasoning

WORKBOOK 1

Non-verbal Reasoning Technique

Dr Stephen C Curran

Edited by Dr Tandip Singh Mann and Andrea Richardson

This book belongs to

ae TUITION

Accelerated Education Publications Ltd

Contents

Pages

1. Elements

1.	Shapes	3-7
2.	Fills	8-11
3.	Lines	12-15
4.	Key Questions used in Non-verbal Reasoning	16-19

2. Movements

1.	Reflection	20-22
2.	Rotation	23-25
3.	Inversion	26-28
4.	Superimposition	29-31
5.	Transposition	32-34

3. Manipulations

1.	Size	35-37
2.	Transformation	38-40
3.	Addition	41-43
4.	Subtraction	44-46
5.	Frequency (Counting)	47-49

4. Patterns

1.	Repetition	50-52
2.	Cumulation	53-55

5. Layering

1.	Level One	56-58
2.	Level Two	59-61
3.	Level Three	62-64
4.	Level Four	65-67
5.	Level Five	68-70

© 2006 Stephen Curran

Chapter One
ELEMENTS

Non-verbal Reasoning questions combine three **Elements**:
Shapes • Fills • Lines

1. Shapes
a. Standard Palette

This comprises all 'closed' geometrically defined shapes.
Triangles • Quadrilaterals • Polygons • Circles

(i) Triangles

Equilateral   Scalene   Isosceles

(ii) Quadrilaterals

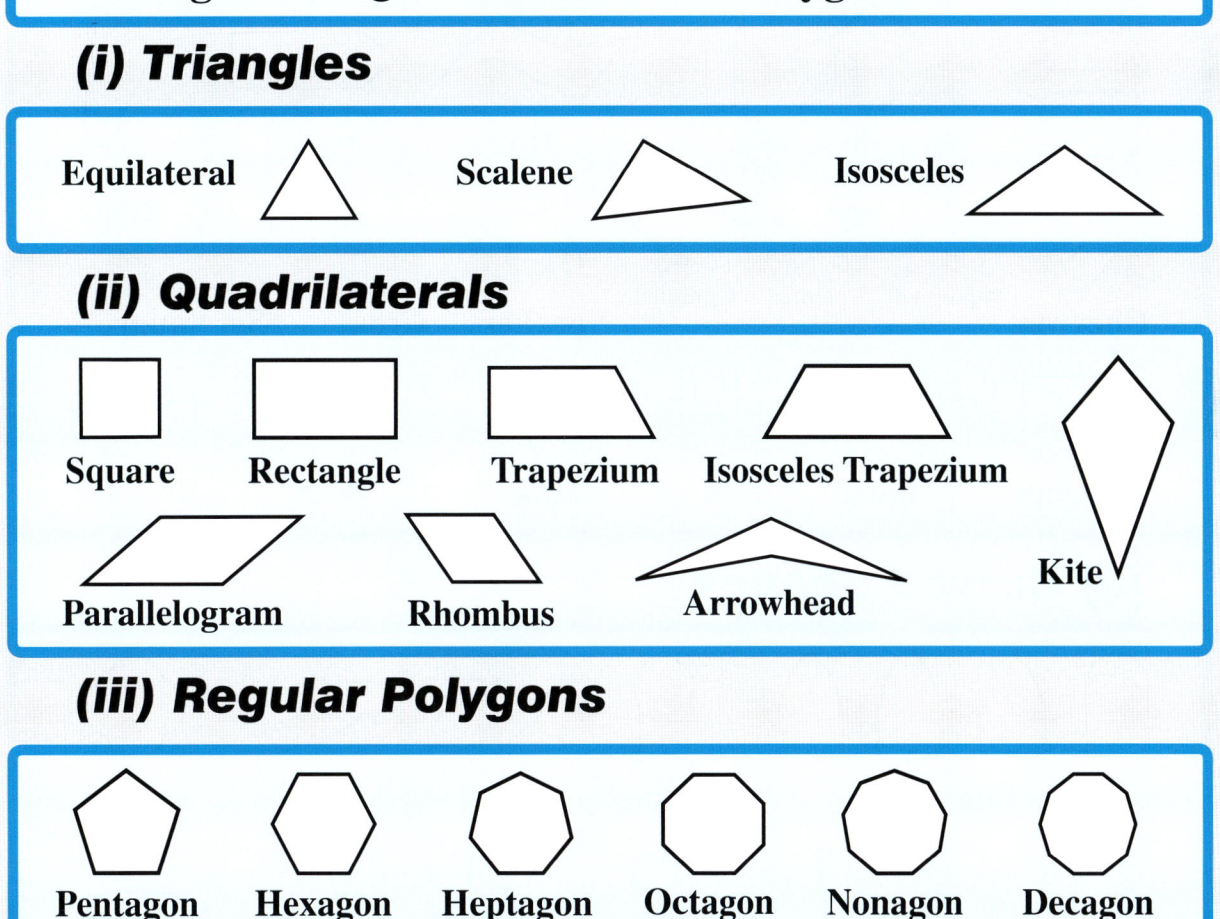

Square   Rectangle   Trapezium   Isosceles Trapezium   Kite

Parallelogram   Rhombus   Arrowhead

(iii) Regular Polygons

Pentagon   Hexagon   Heptagon   Octagon   Nonagon   Decagon

(iv) Circular Shapes

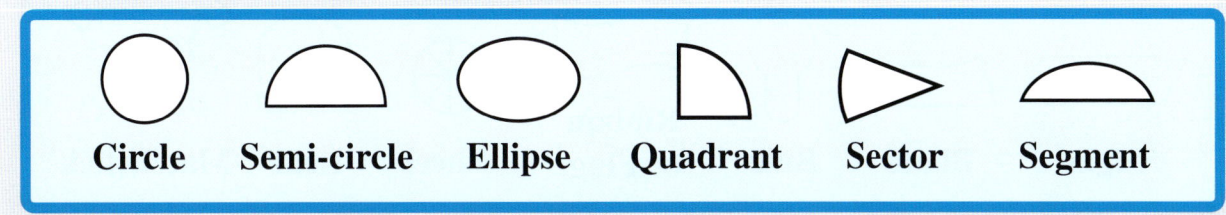

Circle   Semi-circle   Ellipse   Quadrant   Sector   Segment

© 2006 Stephen Curran

(v) Irregular Polygons

Irregular shapes have unequal sides and angles.

General Quadrilateral   Pentagon   Hexagon

b. Specialist Palette

This comprises everyday recognisable 'closed' shapes.

Straight-edged Shapes • Curved Shapes

Other shapes could be shown that are not in these palettes.

(i) Straight-edged Shapes

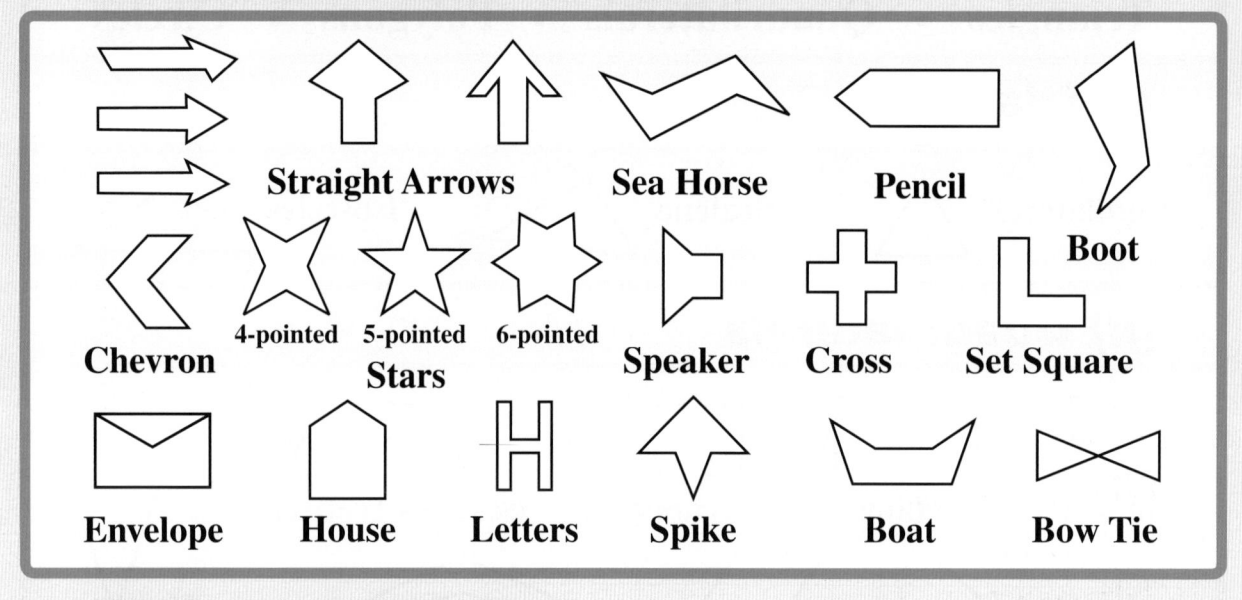

Straight Arrows   Sea Horse   Pencil

Chevron   4-pointed   5-pointed   6-pointed   Speaker   Cross   Set Square
                      Stars   Boot

Envelope   House   Letters   Spike   Boat   Bow Tie

(ii) Curved Shapes

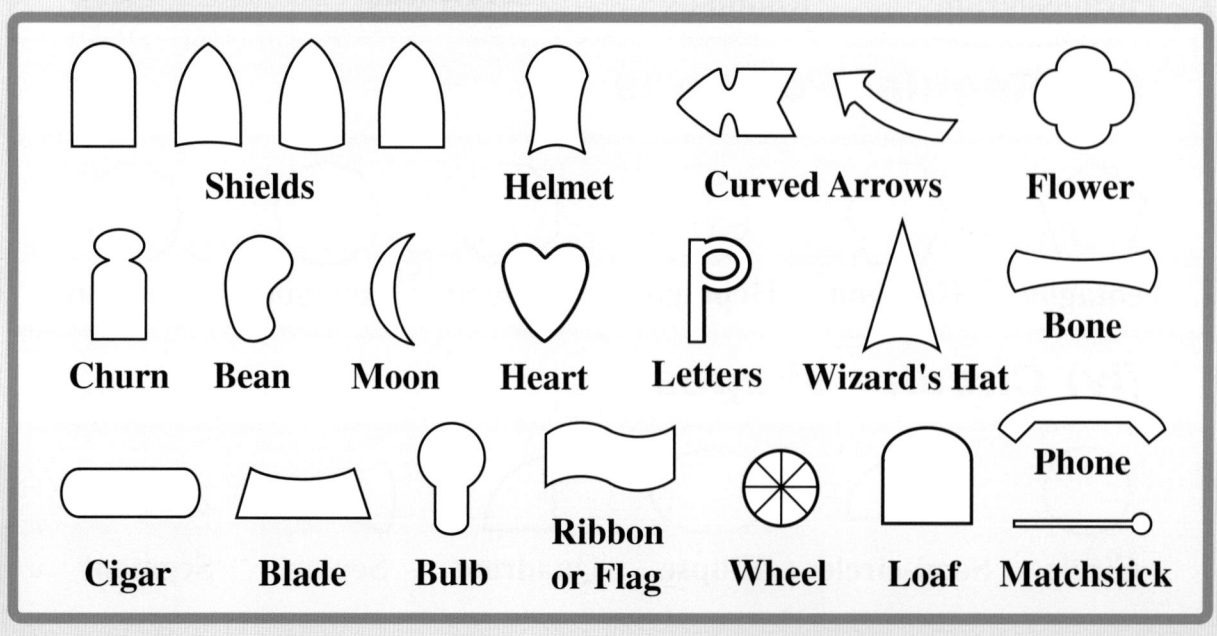

Shields   Helmet   Curved Arrows   Flower

Churn   Bean   Moon   Heart   Letters   Wizard's Hat   Bone

Cigar   Blade   Bulb   Ribbon or Flag   Wheel   Loaf   Phone   Matchstick

© 2006 Stephen Curran

c. Naming Shapes

It is important in Non-verbal Reasoning questions to be able to identify and give **Names to Shapes**. It is much easier to describe what is happening to a shape if it is given a name.

(i) Standard Shapes

Exercise 1: 1   Name the following shapes:

1) 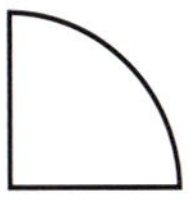   2)    3)    4)

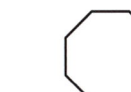

5) 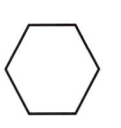   6) 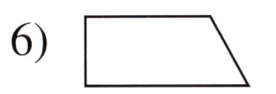   7) 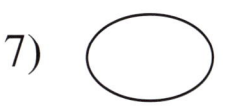   8)

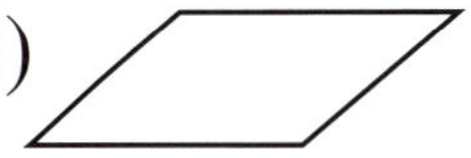

9) 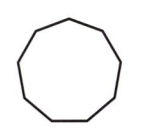   10)

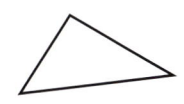

Record scores out of ten here

(ii) Specialist Shapes

Exercise 1: 2   Name the following shapes:

1)    2) 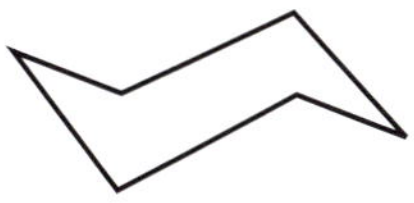   3) 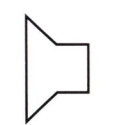   4)

5)    6) 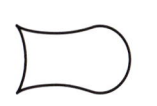   7) 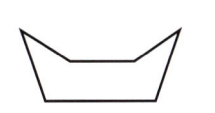   8)

9) 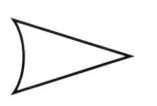   10)

Score

d. Shape Questions

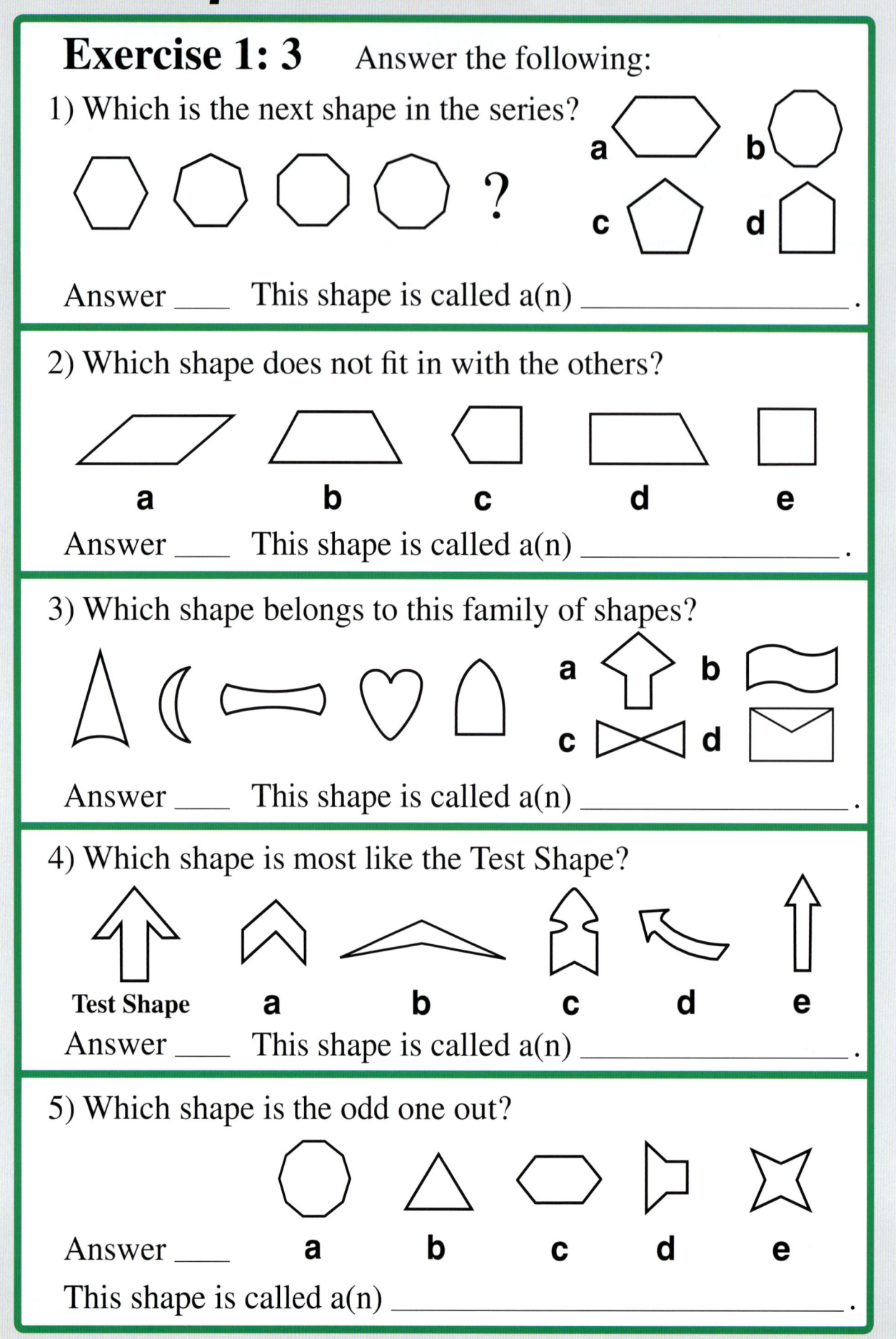

Exercise 1: 3   Answer the following:

1) Which is the next shape in the series?

Answer ____   This shape is called a(n) _____.

2) Which shape does not fit in with the others?

Answer ____   This shape is called a(n) _____.

3) Which shape belongs to this family of shapes?

Answer ____   This shape is called a(n) _____.

4) Which shape is most like the Test Shape?

Test Shape   a   b   c   d   e
Answer ____   This shape is called a(n) _____.

5) Which shape is the odd one out?

Answer ____   a   b   c   d   e
This shape is called a(n) _____.

© 2006 Stephen Curran

6) Which shape does not fit in with these shapes?

a   b   c   d   e

Answer ____   This shape is called a(n) _____.

7) Which shape belongs to this family of shapes?

a   b
c   d

Answer ____   This shape is called a(n) _____.

8) Which shape does not fit in with the others?

a   b   c   d   e

Answer ____   This shape is called a(n) _____.

9) Which is the next shape in the series?

a   b
c   d

Answer ____   This shape is called a(n) _____.

10) Which shape does not fit in with the other shapes?

a   b   c   d   e

Answer ____   This shape is called a(n)
_____.   Score

2. Fills
a. Fill Categories

'Closed' shape **Fills** comprise five different categories:
Block • Shaded • Cross-hatched • Liquid • Dotted

b. Fill Palette
(i) Block Fills

Black   Grey   White

(ii) Shaded Fills

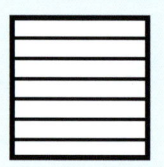

Horizontal Solid Line 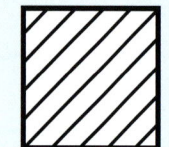   Right Slant Solid Line    Vertical Solid Line    Left Slant Solid Line

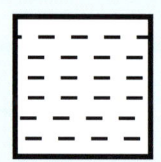

Horizontal Dashed Line 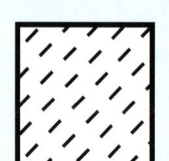   Right Slant Dashed Line 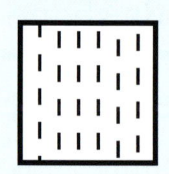   Vertical Dashed Line    Left Slant Dashed Line

(iii) Cross-hatched Fills

Squares   Lattice

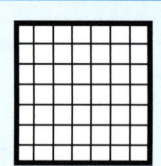

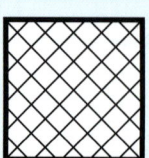

(iv) Liquid Fills

Speckled 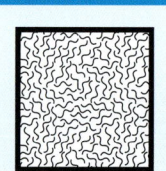   Mottled

(v) Dotted Fills

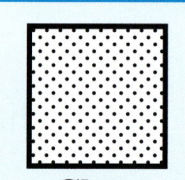

Close 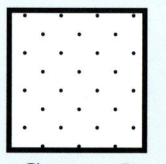   Spaced

© 2006 Stephen Curran

c. Naming Fills

Giving **Names to Fills** also helps when describing shapes.

Exercise 1: 4   Name the following fills:

1)

Fill category: __Block__
Fill type: _____

2)

Fill category: _____
Fill type: __Lattice__

3)

Fill category: _____
Fill type: _____

4)

Fill category: _____
Fill type: _____

5)

Fill category: _____
Fill type: _____

6)

Fill category: _____
Fill type: _____

7)

Fill category: _____
Fill type: _____

8)

Fill category: _____
Fill type: _____

9)

Fill category: _____
Fill type: _____

10)

Fill category: _____
Fill type: _____

Score

d. Fill Questions

Exercise 1: 5   Answer the following:

1) Which shape is next in the series?

Answer ___

Fill category: _____ Fill type: _____

2) Which shape does not fit in with the others?

Answer ___

Fill category: _____ Fill type: _____

3) Which shape is next in the series?

Answer ___

Fill category: _____ Fill type: _____

4) Which shape does not fit in with the others?

Answer ___

Fill category: _____ Fill type: _____

5) Which shape is next in the series?

Answer ___

Fill category: _____ Fill type: _____

6) Which two shapes are most alike?

Answer ___ and ___

a　b　c　d　e

Fill category: _____ Fill type: _____

7) Which shape is the odd one out?

Answer ___

a　b　c　d　e

Fill category: _____ Fill type: _____

8) Which shape is most like the Test Shape?

Test Shape　a　b　c　d　e

Fill category: _____

Answer ___　Fill type: _____

9) Which is the next shape in the series?

Answer ___

a　b　c　d

Fill category: _____ Fill type: _____

10) Which shape is most like the Test Shape?

Test Shape　a　b　c　d　e

Answer ___

Fill category: _____

Fill type: _____

Score

3. Lines
a. Line Palette

All **Line Types** have three main properties:
1. Solid — Dashed — Dotted
2. Straight — Curved
3. Thin — Thick

For example, this Line Type is described as: Dotted, Curved, Thick

b. Line Shape Palette

This comprises everyday recognisable 'open' **Line Shapes**.
Straight-edged Shapes • **Curved Shapes**
This palette is not exhaustive as other shapes also exist.

(i) Straight-edged Shapes

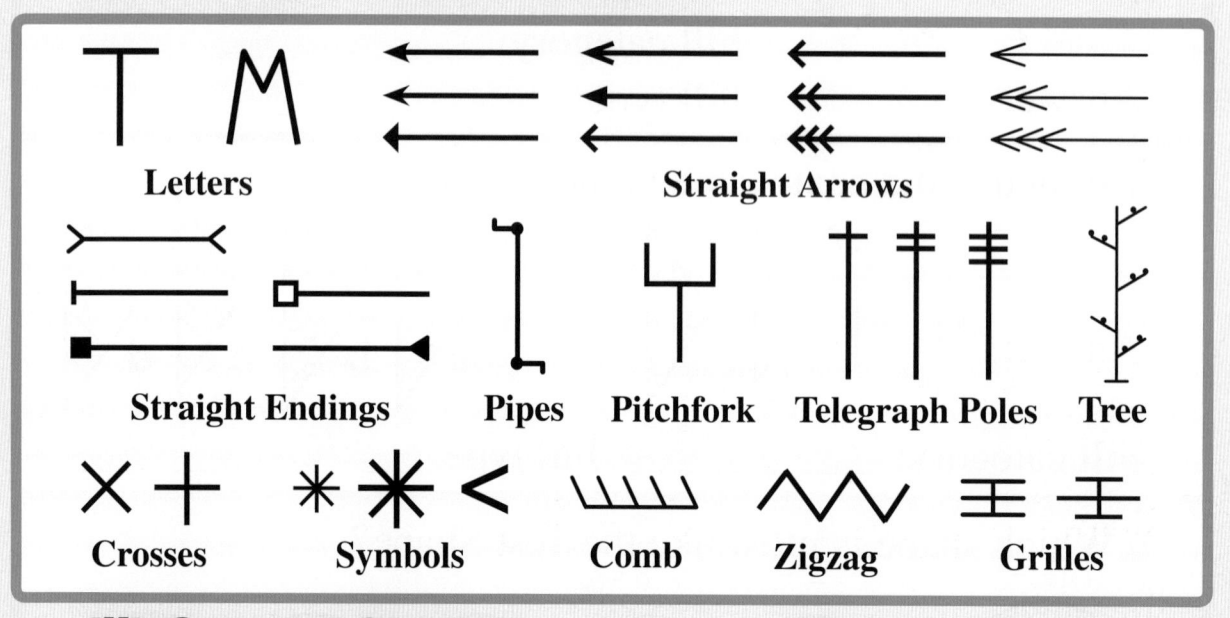

Letters • Straight Arrows

Straight Endings • Pipes • Pitchfork • Telegraph Poles • Tree

Crosses • Symbols • Comb • Zigzag • Grilles

(ii) Curved Shapes

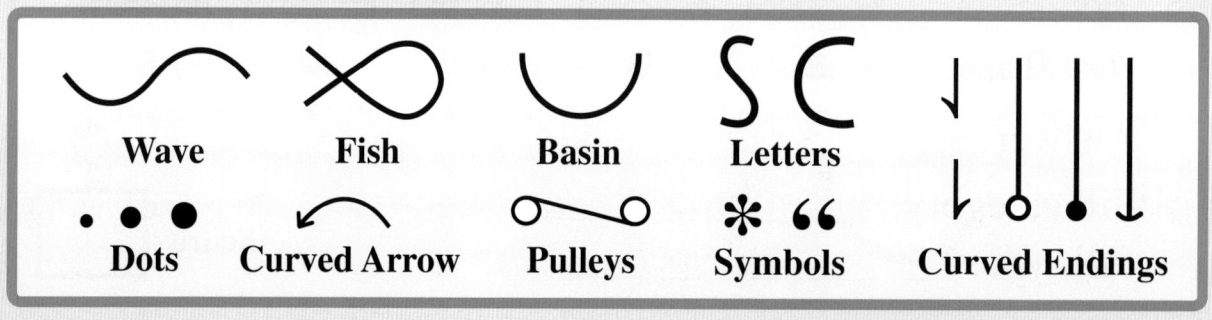

Wave • Fish • Basin • Letters

Dots • Curved Arrow • Pulleys • Symbols • Curved Endings

© 2006 Stephen Curran

c. Naming Lines

Naming Lines and Line Shapes helps with identification.

(i) Straight-edged Shapes

Exercise 1: 6a   Identify the following line types:

1)
Type: _Dotted_ _Straight_ _Thin_
Shape: _____

2) 
Type: _____ _____ _____
Shape: _Symbol_

3) 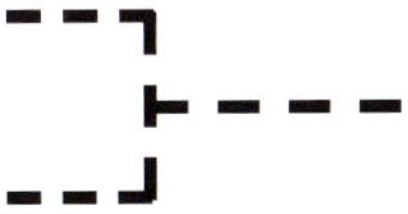
Type: _____ _____ _____
Shape: _____

4) 
Type: _____ _____ _____
Shape: _____

5) 
Type: _____ _____ _____
Shape: _____

(ii) Curved Shapes

Exercise 1: 6b   Identify the following line types:

6) 
Type: _____ _____ _____
Shape: _____

7) 
Type: _____ _____ _____
Shape: _____

8) 
Type: _____ _____ _____
Shape: _____

9) 
Type: _____ _____ _____
Shape: _____

10) 
Type: _____ _____ _____
Shape: _____

Score

d. Line Questions

Exercise 1: 7   Answer the following:

1) Which is the next figure in the series?

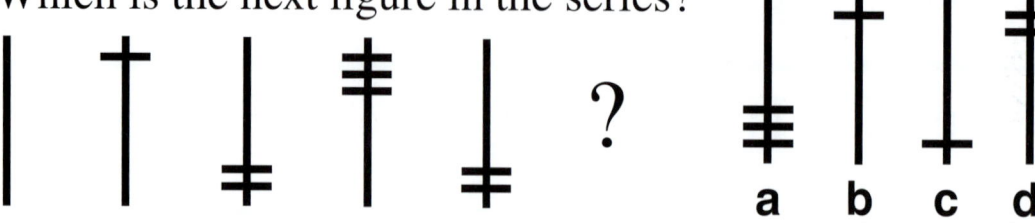

Answer ___   These figures are called _____.

2) Which figure does not fit in with the others?

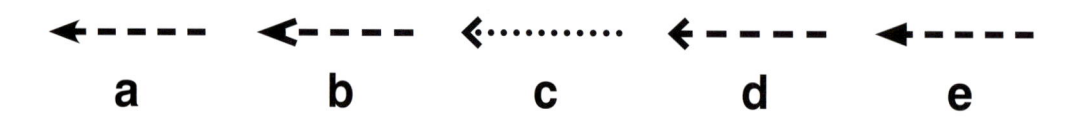

Answer ___   These figures are called _____.

3) Which figure belongs to this family of figures?

Answer ___   This figure is called a(n) _____.

4) Which figure is most like the Test Figure?

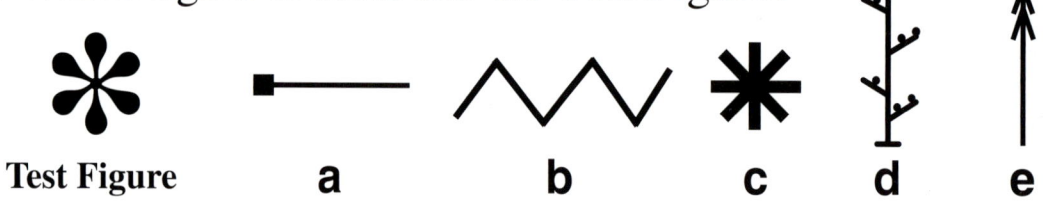

Answer ___   This figure is called a(n) _____.

5) Which figure is the odd one out?

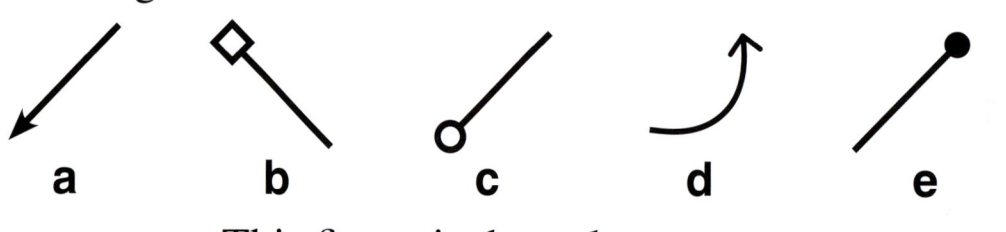

Answer ___   This figure is the only _____.

6) Which figure does not fit in with the other figures?

a   b   c   d   e

Answer ____   This line type is: _____ _____ _____

7) Which figure belongs to this family of figures?

a   b
c   d

Answer ____   This line type is: _____ _____ _____

8) Which figure does not fit in with the others?

a   b   c   d   e

Answer ____   This line type is: _____ _____ _____

9) Which figure is next in the series?

a   b
c   d

Answer ____   These figures are Curved _____.

10) Which figure belongs to this family of figures?

a   b
c   d

Answer ____
The line type is:
_____ _____ _____

Score

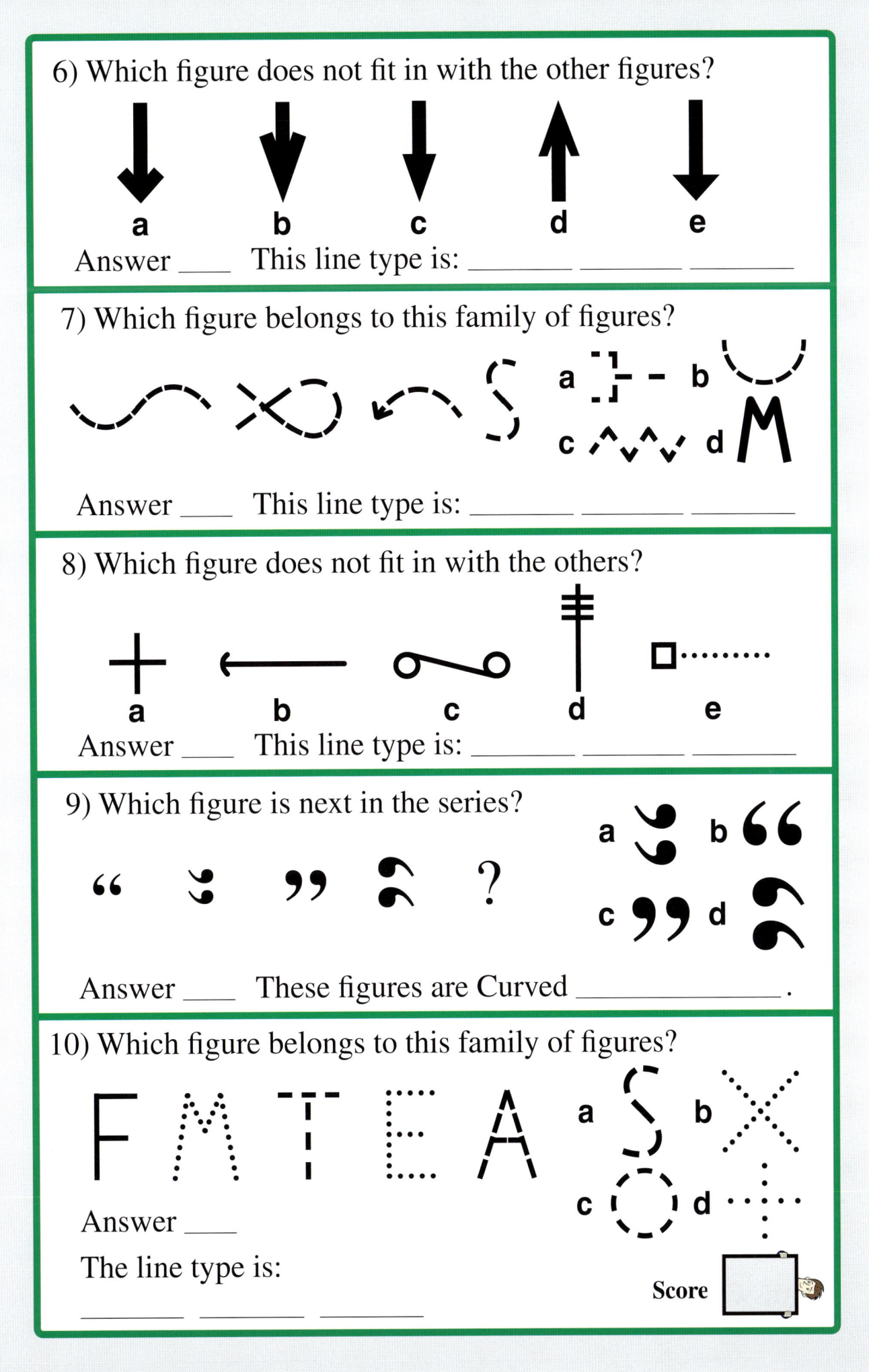

4. Key Questions used in Non-verbal Reasoning

All Non-verbal Reasoning questions are centred around just three key areas. It is important to be able to identify:

Similarity • Difference • Pattern

These questions have already been used in this book:
1) Which shape is most similar to the shape given?
2) Which shape is most different from the shape given?
3) Which shape is the next shape in the series?

a. Similarity

Shapes are **Similar** if they are like each other in some way. This likeness can apply to any aspect of the shape or shapes.

These two shapes are identical, except they are of a different size and fill type. The second shape has also been rotated 45° in a Clockwise direction in relation to the first shape.

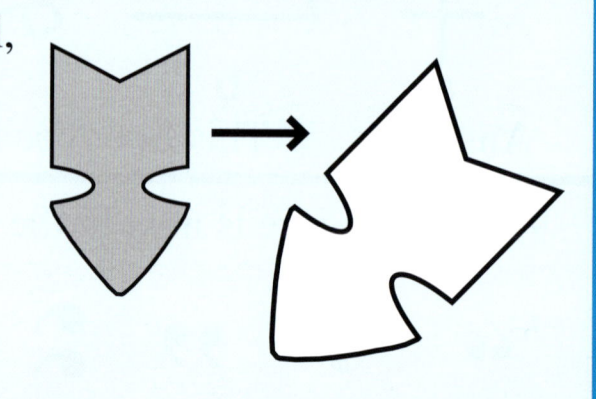

Similarity involves identifying one or more common characteristics between shapes.

Example: Which shape is most similar to the Test Shape?

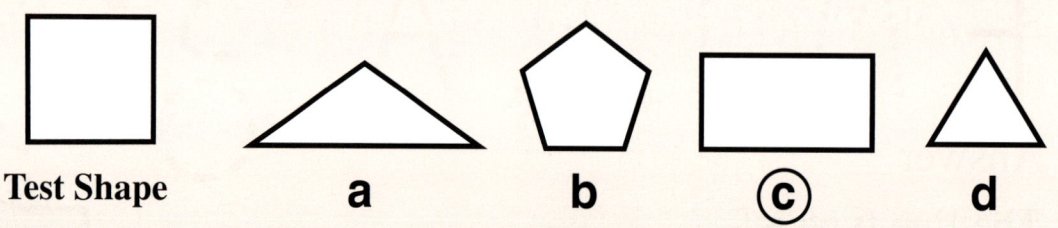

Test Shape   a   b   c   d

Answer: Shape **c** is most similar as it has four sides.

b. Difference

Shapes are **Different** if they are unlike each other in some way. Difference can mean the shape or shapes have no likeness at all, or there are one or more aspects not alike.

Both these shapes are Stars with the same fill type but they have a different number of sides.

Difference involves spotting the shape most unlike the rest.

Example: Which shape is different from the other shapes?

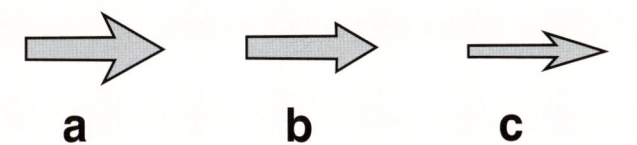

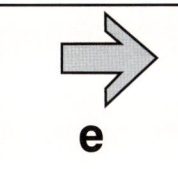

a b c d e

Answer: Shape **d** is different because it has a Black Fill.

c. Pattern

A **Repetitive** or **Cumulative Pattern** can be established in a series or sequence of shapes or figures (see pages 50-55).

The fill changes from Grey to White to Grey repetitively. One more Circle with a Black Fill is added each time cumulatively.

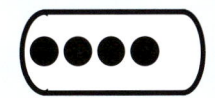

A pattern is identified by spotting repetition or cumulation.

Example: Which shape is next in the series?

a b c d

Answer: Shape **c** is next because it is bigger and it has a White Fill.

© 2006 Stephen Curran

Exercise 1: 8   Answer the following:

1) Which is the next shape in the series?

Answer ____   Why? _____

2) Which shape does not fit in with the others?

Answer ____   Why not? _____

3) Which shape is next in the series?

Answer ____   Why? _____

4) Which shape does not fit in with the others?

Answer ____   Why not? _____

5) Which is the next shape in the series?

Answer ____   Why? _____

© 2006 Stephen Curran

6) Which two shapes are most alike?

a b c d e

Answer ____ and ____   Why? _____

_____

7) Which shape is the odd one out?

a b c d e

Answer ____   Why? _____

_____

8) Which shape is most similar to the Test Shape?

Test Shape   a b c d e

Answer ____   Why? _____

_____

9) Which shape is next in the series?

a b c d

Answer ____   Why? _____

_____

10) Which shape is most like the Test Shape?

Test Shape   a b c d e

Score

Answer ____   Why? _____

_____

© 2006 Stephen Curran

Chapter Two
MOVEMENTS

In Non-verbal Reasoning, shapes can **Move** in five ways:
Reflection • Rotation • Inversion
Superimposition • Transposition

1. Reflection

A shape can be **Reflected** across an imaginary Mirror Line or Line of Reflection. Shape **A** is reflected the other side of the Mirror Line to form shape **B**.

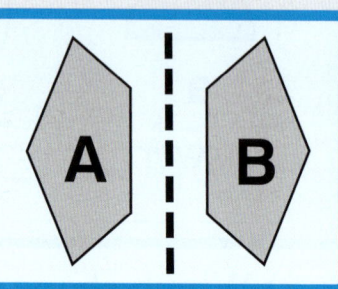

Key Non-verbal Reasoning questions apply to reflections:

Example 1: Which shape is a reflection of the Test Shape?

Test Shape   a   b   ⓒ   d   e

Answer: **c** is a reflection of the Test Shape.

Example 2: Which pair of shapes are not reflections?

a   ⓑ   c   d

Answer: **b** - The Slanted Shaded Fills are not reflections.

Example 3: Which is the next shape in the series?

a   b   ⓒ   d

Answer: **c** - The shape reflects correctly and has the correct Liquid Fill type.

Exercise 2: 1   Answer the following:

1) Which is the next figure in the series?

Answer ____   Fill category: _____
              Fill type: _____

2) Which pair of shapes does not fit in with the others?

Answer ____   These shapes are called _____ .

3) Which is the next figure in the series?

              Fill category: _____
Answer ____   Fill type: _____

4) Which figure does not fit in with the others?

              Why not? _____
Answer ____   _____

5) Which letter is next in the series?

Y A C D E H I ?   a L   b K
                    c M   d B

Answer ____   Why? _____
_____

© 2006 Stephen Curran   21

6) Which two pairs of shapes are most alike?

a   b   c   d   e

Answer ___ and ___   Why? _____

7) Which pair of shapes is the odd one out?

a   b   c   d   e

Answer ___   i) Why? _____
ii) These shapes are called _____.

8) Which figure is a reflection of the Test Figure?

Test Figure   a   b   c   d   e

Answer ___   The inner shape is called a(n) _____.

9) Which is the next shape in the series?

a   b   c   d

What is this shape called?

Answer ___   _____

10) Which figure is a reflection of the Test Figure?

Test Figure   a   b   c   d   e

Answer ___   The outer shape is called a(n) _____.

Score

22   © 2006 Stephen Curran

2. Rotation

In Non-verbal Reasoning, shapes can **Rotate** in a Clockwise or Anticlockwise direction.

To avoid confusion it is best to measure the rotation by the shortest route. This will be in either a **Clockwise** or an **Anticlockwise** direction around the **360°** turn. There are three main rotations:

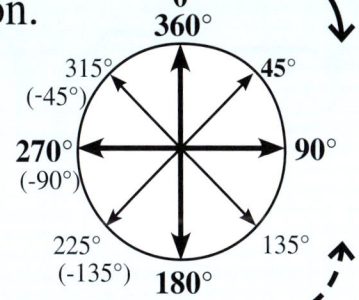

$45° (\frac{1}{8})$ turn $90° (\frac{1}{4})$ turn $180° (\frac{1}{2})$ turn

Smaller shapes can rotate around the outside of larger shapes or on the inside of larger shapes.

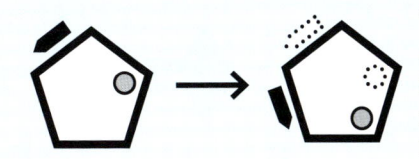

The Pencil Shape has moved Anticlockwise around the Pentagon and the Circle has moved Clockwise within the Pentagon.

Key Non-verbal Reasoning questions apply to rotations:

Example 1: Which shape completes the second pair of shapes?

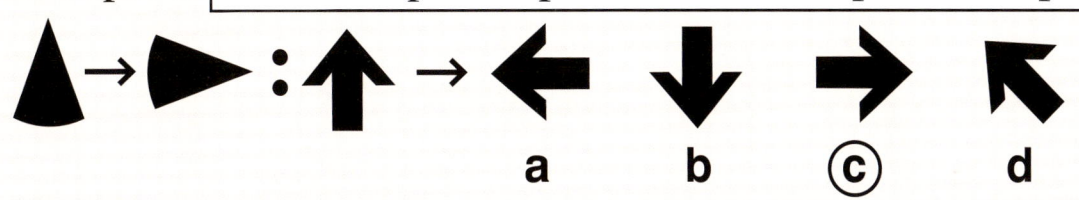

Answer: **c** - It has rotated 90° Clockwise (in the same way as the first pair).

Example 2: Which rotation is the odd one out?

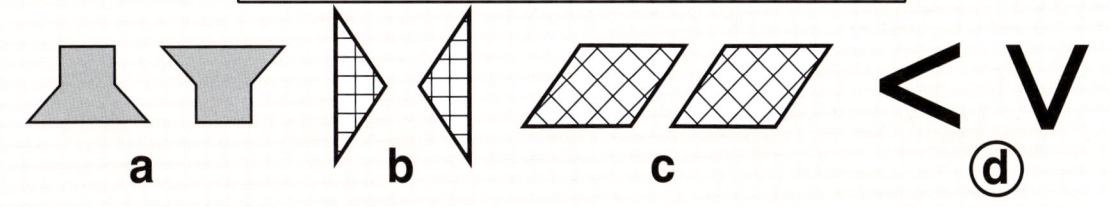

Answer: **d** - It has rotated 90° Anticlockwise but should rotate 180°.

Example 3: Which figure is next in the series?

Answer: **d** - The Arrow rotates 45° Anticlockwise; the next Arrow must have a Black Fill; the Circle rotates 45° Clockwise around the centre (or 90° Clockwise around the Arrow).

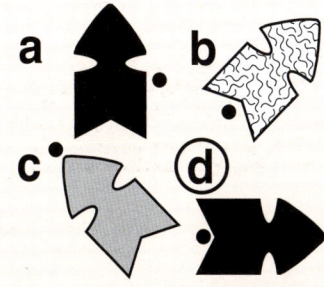

© 2006 Stephen Curran

Exercise 2: 2   Answer the following:

1) Which is the next figure in the series?

Answer _____   The Hexagon has been rotated Clockwise _____°.
The Ellipse rotates around the Hexagon in a(n) _____ direction.

2) Which pair of shapes does not rotate like the Test Shapes?

Test Shapes

Answer _____   The shape has been rotated _____°.

3) Which shape rotates in the same way as the Test Shapes?

Test Shapes
Answer _____   The shape has been rotated _____° _____.

4) Which figure is most like the Test Figure?

Test Figure

Answer _____   In comparison with the outer shape the inner shapes have rotated _____° and _____°.

5) Which figure is the odd one out?

Answer _____   It rotates in a(n) _____ direction.

© 2006 Stephen Curran

6) Which figure does not fit in with the other figures?

a b c d e

Answer ____   Why not? _____

7) Which shape belongs to this family of shapes?

a b c d

Why? _____

Answer ____   _____

8) Which pair of shapes does not rotate like the Test Shapes?

Test Shapes   a   b   c

Answer ____   This shape has been rotated _____°.

9) Which figure is next in the series?

a b c d

Answer ____   The Flower Shape rotates _____°.
The Moon Shape rotates _____° _____ around the Flower.

10) Which letter is missing from this family of letters?

D E G J K L M   a F   b N
                  c O   d H

Answer ____   Why? _____
_____

Score

© 2006 Stephen Curran

3. Inversion

In Non-verbal Reasoning, a shape can be **Inverted** (Flipped) Horizontally or Vertically or in both directions at the same time:

1. Vertical Inversion/Flip

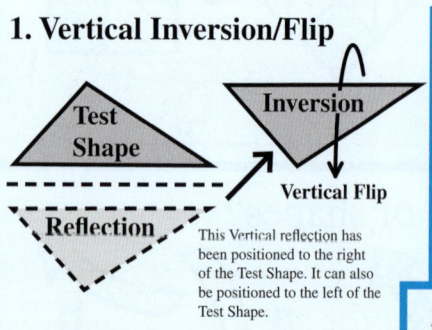

This Vertical reflection has been positioned to the right of the Test Shape. It can also be positioned to the left of the Test Shape.

Vertical Inversion can be understood as a Vertical reflection positioned to the right or left side of the original shape. It can also be seen as a Vertical Flip.

2. Horizontal Inversion/Flip

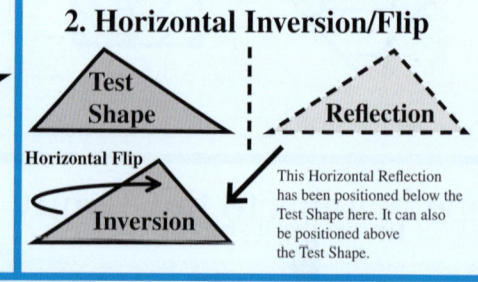

This Horizontal Reflection has been positioned below the Test Shape here. It can also be positioned above the Test Shape.

Horizontal Inversion can be understood as a Horizontal reflection positioned underneath or above the original shape. It can also be seen as a Horizontal Flip.

3. Vertical and Horizontal Inversion/Double Flip

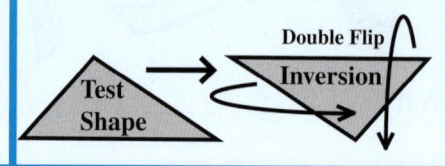

Combined Vertical and Horizontal Inversion or Flip is a 180° rotation of the original shape.

Key Non-verbal Reasoning questions apply to inversions:

Example 1: Which figure is most similar to the Test Figure?

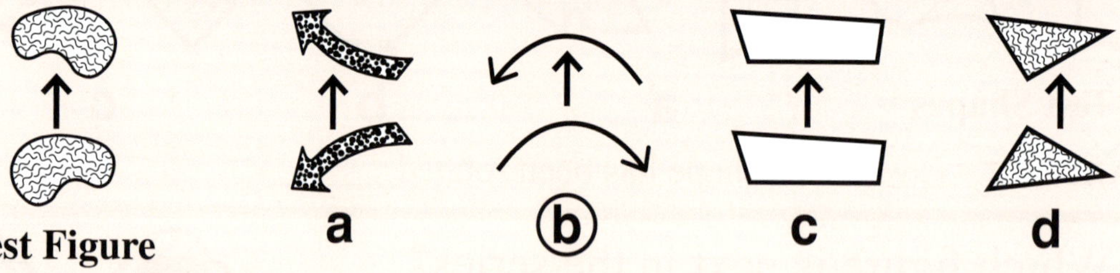

Answer: **b** - This is a Horizontal inversion/flip. (Horizontal reflection positioned above the original shape.)

Example 2: Which shape is next in the series?

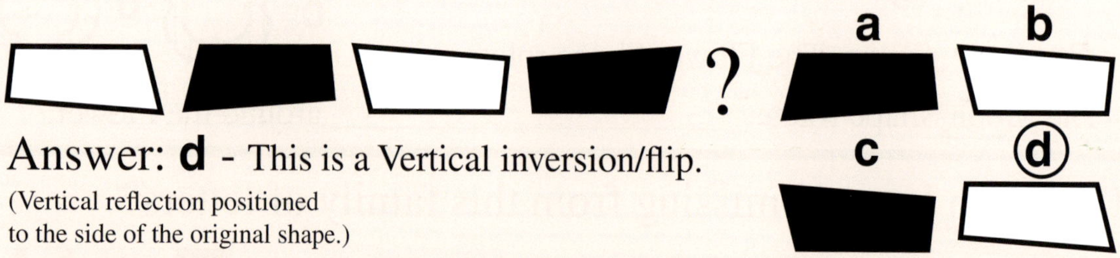

Answer: **d** - This is a Vertical inversion/flip. (Vertical reflection positioned to the side of the original shape.)

Example 3: Which pair of shapes is the odd one out?

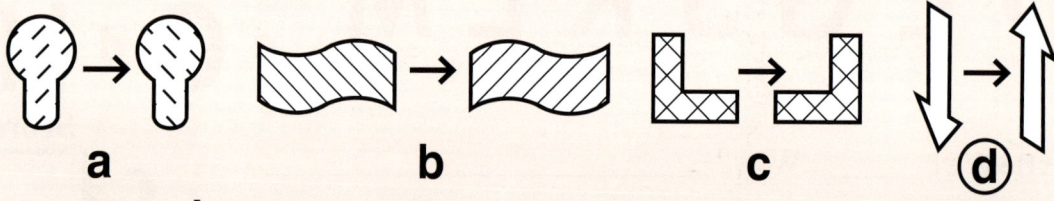

Answer: **d** - This is a Horizontal and Vertical inversion (rotated 180°).

Exercise 2: 3 Answer the following:

1) Which shape is next in the series?

Answer ____   Inversion type? ___Vertical inversion/flip___

2) Which shape does not fit in with the others?

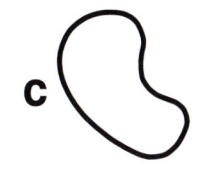

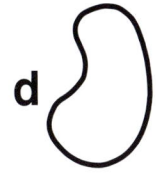

Why not? _____
Answer ____

3) Which is the next shape in the series?

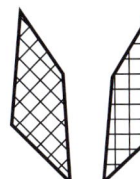

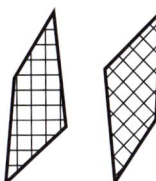

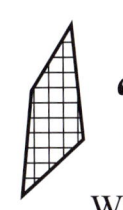

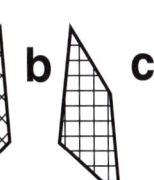

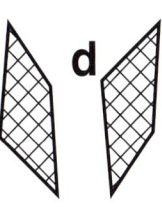

Why? _____
Answer ____

4) Which pair of shapes does not fit in with the others?

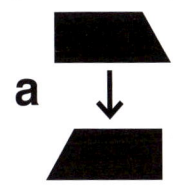

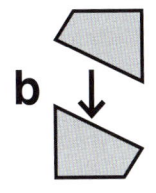

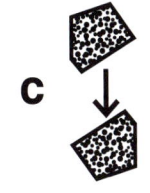

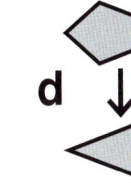

Why not? _____
Answer ____

5) Which shape is next in the series?

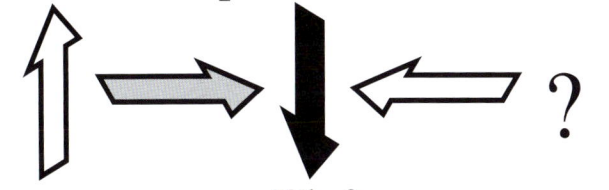

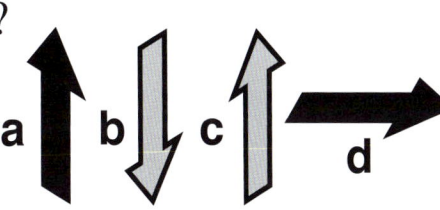

Why? _____
Answer ____

© 2006 Stephen Curran   27

6) Which two shapes are most similar?

a b c d e

Answer ___ and ___   Why? _____

7) Which figure is the odd one out?

a b c d e

Answer ___   Why? _____

8) Which figure is most unlike the Test Figure?

Test Figure   a b c d e

Answer ___   Why? _____

9) Which is the next shape in the series?

a b c d

Answer ___   Why? _____

10) Which pair of figures is most like the Test Figures?

Test Figures   a b c d

Answer ___   Why? _____

Score

4. Superimposition

In Non-verbal Reasoning, shapes can be **Superimposed** onto other shapes. These superimpositions can include a **Merger**, an **Overlay**, a **Linkage** or an **Enclosure**.

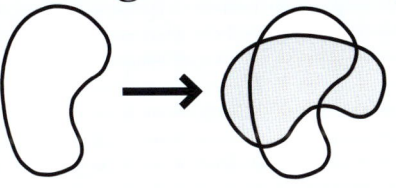

	1. Merger	**2. Overlay**	**3. Linkage**	**4. Enclosure**
Superimpositions have been indicated with a Grey Fill to help with visual clarity and ease of understanding.	The second shape Merges (crosses over) the first shape. The integrity (lines) of both shapes is retained. In this case it is a 90° rotation and inversion of the original shape.	The second shape Overlays (is on top of) the first shape. The original shape can be fully or partially covered. In this case it is a 90° rotation of the original shape.	The second shape is Linked to (does not cross over) the first shape. The integrity (lines) of both shapes is kept. Several shapes can be Linked together.	The second shape is Enclosed within the first shape. In this case a copy of the first shape is reduced in size and Enclosed within the original shape.

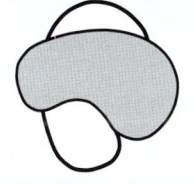

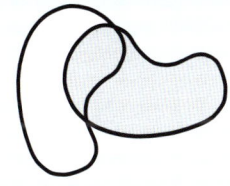

Key Non-verbal Reasoning questions use superimpositions:

Example 1: Which figure is most similar to the Test Figure?

Test Figure   **a**   **b**   **c**   **d**

Answer: **d** - This is a rotated superimposed merger of 90°.

Example 2: Which superimposition is the odd one out?

a   **b**   **c**   **d**   **e**

Answer: **c** - The enclosed shape has not been rotated 180°.

Example 3: Which superimposition is next in the series?

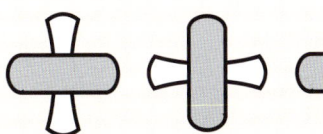

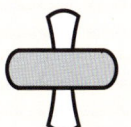

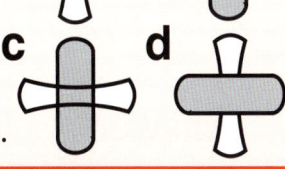

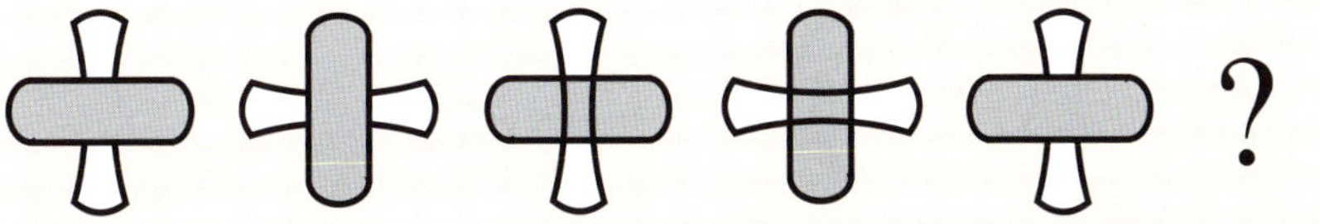

Answer: **b** - The previous figure has been rotated 90°. The Cigar Shape with a Grey Fill overlays the Bone Shape.

© 2006 Stephen Curran

Exercise 2: 4   Answer the following:

1) Which is the next figure in the series?

Superimposition type: _____

Answer ____

2) Which figure does not fit in with the others?

a   b   c   d   e

Answer ____   Superimposition type: _____

3) Which figure belongs to this family of figures?

Superimposition type: _____

Answer ____

4) Which figure is most like the Test Figure?

Test Figure   a   b   c   d

Answer ____   Superimposition type: _____

5) Which figure is the odd one out?

a   b   c   d   e

Answer ____   Superimposition type: _____

6) Which figure does not fit in with the others?

a   b   c   d

Answer ____
Superimposition types: _____ and _____

7) Which figure belongs to this family of figures?

a   b   c   d

Superimposition type: _____
Answer ____

8) Which figure does not fit in with the other figures?

a   b   c   d   e

Answer ____   Superimposition type: _____

9) Which figure is next in the series?

a   b   c   d

Superimposition type: _____
Answer ____

10) Which figure belongs to this family of figures?

a   b   c   d

Answer ____
Superimposition types:
_____/_____/_____

Score

© 2006 Stephen Curran

31

5. Transposition

In Non-verbal Reasoning, shapes can be **Transposed** or **Moved** from one position to another, either Horizontally or Vertically. Movements to the right or left are Horizontal, and movements up or down are Vertical. Some transpositions involve both Vertical and Horizontal movements, i.e. a shape could move up and to the right.

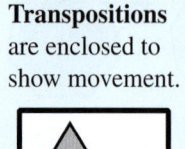

Transpositions are enclosed to show movement.

1. Horizontal Transposition

2. Vertical Transposition

3. Horizontal and Vertical Transposition

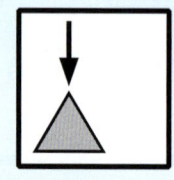

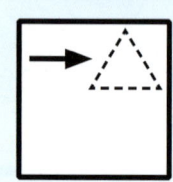

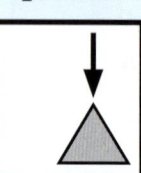

Key Non-verbal Reasoning questions use transpositions:

Example 1: Which figure is most similar to the Test Figure?

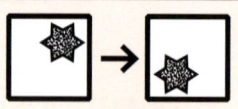

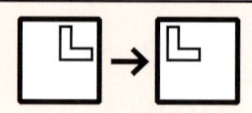

Test Figure   a   ⓑ   c

Answer: **b** - It is a Vertical and Horizontal transposition.

Example 2: Which transposition is the odd one out?

ⓐ   b   c   d

Answer: **a** - It is a Horizontal transposition.

Example 3: Which transposition is next in the series?

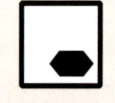

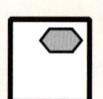

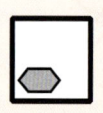

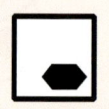

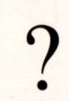

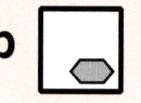

Answer: **c** - The Hexagon changes to a Grey Fill and transposes Vertically.

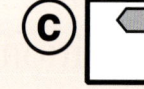

Exercise 2: 5   Answer the following:

1) Which figure is next in the series?

Answer ____   Transposition types:
Grey Fill: _Horizontal_   White: _____   Black: _____

2) Which figure completes the second pair of figures?

Transposition types: Flower: _____
Answer ____   Straight Arrow: _____   Circle: _____

3) Which is the next figure in the series?

Answer ____   Transposition types:
Circle: _____   Pentagon: _____

4) Which pair of figures does not fit in with the others?

Transposition type:
Answer ____   _____ and _____

5) Which is the next figure in the series?

Transposition types:
Answer ____   Octagon: _____   Kite: _____

© 2006 Stephen Curran

33

6) Which figure completes the second pair of figures?

Answer ____   Transposition types: Curved Arrow: _____
F Shape: _____ and _____

7) Which pair of figures is the odd one out?

Answer ____   Transposition type: _____

8) Which pair of figures is most like the Test Figures?

Answer ____   Transposition types:
Black Shape: _____ Grey Shape: _____

9) Which figure is next in the series?

Answer ____
Transposition type: _____

10) Which pair of figures is most like the Test Figures?

Answer ____
Transposition types:
_____ and _____

Score

Chapter Three
MANIPULATIONS

In Non-verbal Reasoning, shapes can be **Manipulated** by:
Size • Transformation • Addition • Subtraction • Frequency

1. Size

Shapes can **Increase** in size or **Decrease** in size:

1. Enlargement **2. Reduction**

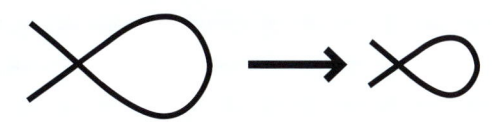

Key Non-verbal Reasoning questions apply to size change:

Example 1: Which shape completes the second pair of shapes?

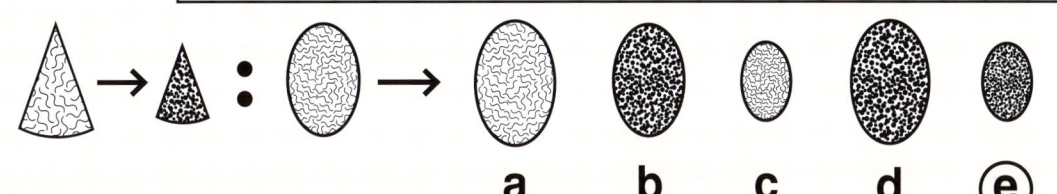

Answer: Shape **e** is a reduction and has a Speckled Fill.

Example 2: Which shape is different from the others?

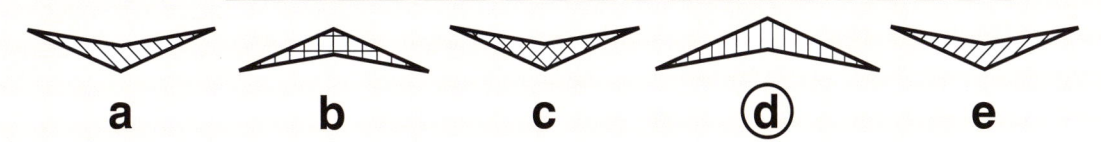

Answer: Shape **d** is an enlargement of the other shapes.

Example 3: Which shape is next in the series?

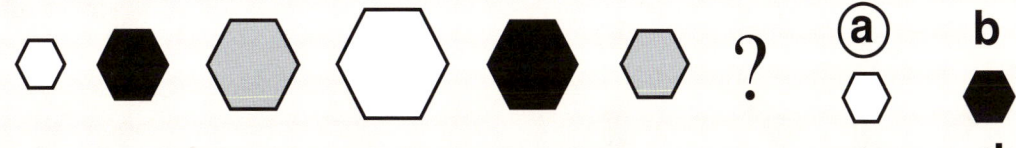

Answer: Shape **a** is a reduction (the next smallest) and has the correct fill.

Exercise 3: 1 Answer the following:

1) Which is the next figure in the series?

Answer ____

The change of size is a(n) __Enlargement__ .

2) Which shape does not fit in with the others?

Answer ____ The change of size is a(n) _____ .

3) Which pair of figures is most similar to the Test Figures?

Test Figures

Answer ____ Name the shapes:
The _____ Shape reduces.
The _____ Shape enlarges.

4) Which pair of figures is most like the Test Figures?

Test Figures

Answer ____ The change of size is a(n) _____ .

5) Which is the next figure in the series?

Answer ____ The change of size is a(n) _____ .

36 © 2006 Stephen Curran

6) Which pair of figures does not fit in with the other figures?

a   b   c   d

Answer ____   The change of size is a(n) _____.

7) Which figure belongs to this family of figures?

a   b   c   d

Answer ____

The enclosed shape is a(n) _____ of the outer shape.

8) Which figure does not fit in with the others?

a   b   c   d   e

Answer ____   The change of size is a(n) _____.

9) Which figure is the odd one out?

a   b   c

Answer ____   The change of size is a(n) _____.

10) Which figure belongs to this family of figures?

a   b   c   d

Answer ____

If the enclosed Triangles are placed in size order, largest to smallest, each one would be a(n) _____ of the previous Triangle.

Score

2. Transformation

In Non-verbal Reasoning, shapes can be **Transformed**. This means a shape can be **Stretched** or **Squashed** but retains its main characteristics, i.e. the same number of sides and vertices (corners) and one dimension must remain constant.

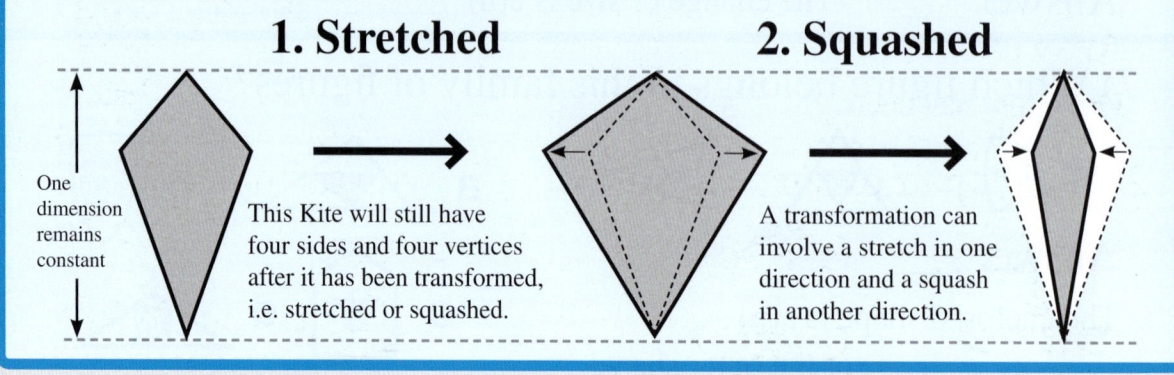

1. Stretched

One dimension remains constant

This Kite will still have four sides and four vertices after it has been transformed, i.e. stretched or squashed.

2. Squashed

A transformation can involve a stretch in one direction and a squash in another direction.

Key Non-verbal Reasoning questions apply to transformations:

Example 1: Which shape is a transformation of the Test Shape?

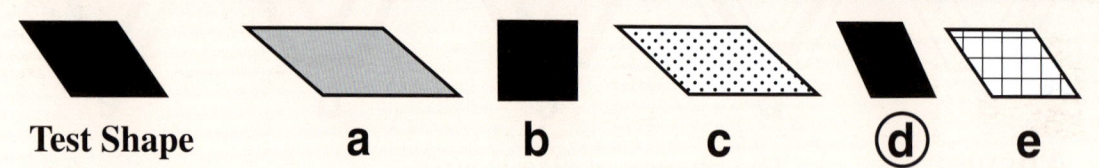

Test Shape   a   b   c   ⓓ   e

Answer: **d** is a squashed Parallelogram with a Black Fill.

Example 2: Which pair of shapes are not transformations?

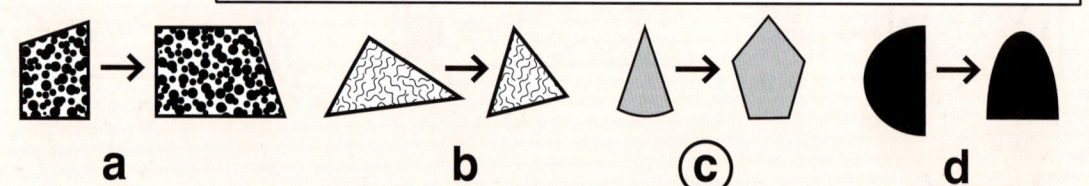

a   b   ⓒ   d

Answer: **c** as the shapes are different and not transformed.

Example 3: Which shape is next in the series?

? a ⓑ c d

Answer: **b** has been stretched and has the correct Grey Fill.

38 © 2006 Stephen Curran

Exercise 3: 2   Answer the following:

1) Which is the next figure in the series?

Answer ____

The figure has been __Squashed__ .

2) Which pair of shapes does not fit in with the others?

a   b   c   d   e

Answer ____   The shape has been _____ .

3) Which is the next figure in the series?

Answer ____

The House Shape has been _____ .
The Cross Shape has been _____ .

4) Which figure is the odd one out?

a   b   c   d   e

Answer ____   The _____ Shape has been squashed.

5) Which figure is next in the series?

Answer ____   The _____ Shape has been stretched.

6) Which two figures are most similar?

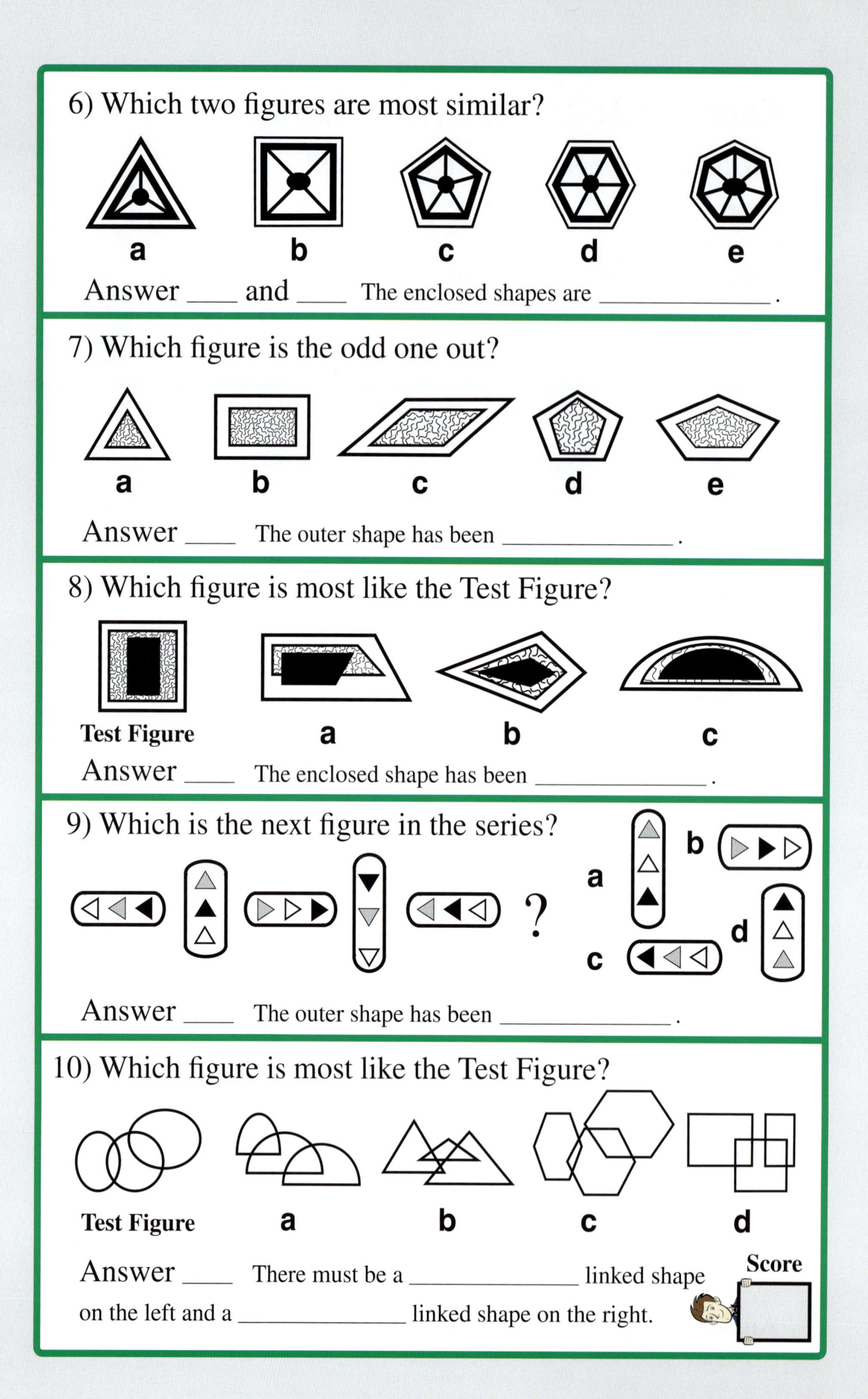

a   b   c   d   e

Answer ____ and ____ The enclosed shapes are _____.

7) Which figure is the odd one out?

a   b   c   d   e

Answer ____ The outer shape has been _____.

8) Which figure is most like the Test Figure?

Test Figure   a   b   c

Answer ____ The enclosed shape has been _____.

9) Which is the next figure in the series?

a   b   c   d

Answer ____ The outer shape has been _____.

10) Which figure is most like the Test Figure?

Test Figure   a   b   c   d

Answer ____ There must be a _____ linked shape on the left and a _____ linked shape on the right.

Score

3. Addition

In Non-verbal Reasoning, one or more shapes can be **Added** to the original shape or separate additional shapes can be added.

1. Additions to shapes

The original shape has been copied, rotated 90° and superimposed onto the original shape. Additions are often combined with rotations, reflections, superimpositions and inversions.

2. Additional shapes

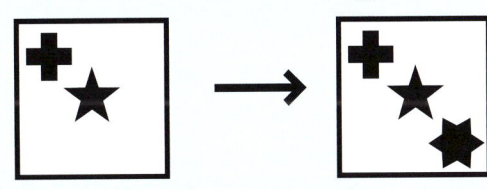

A third shape has been added to the two original shapes. This can also be understood as a change in Frequency (see pages 47-49).

Key Non-verbal Reasoning questions apply to additions:

Example 1: Which shape has an addition to the Test Shape?

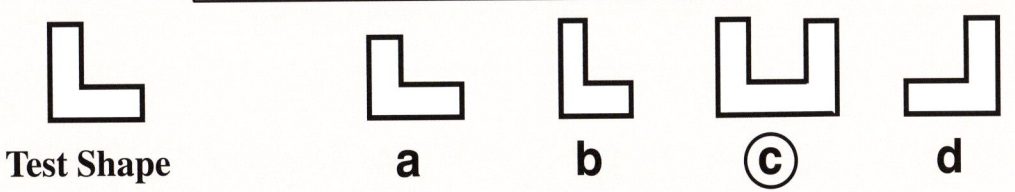

Test Shape   a   b   ⓒ   d

Answer: **c** - The original shape has received an addition.

Example 2: Which shape has no additions to the Test Shape?

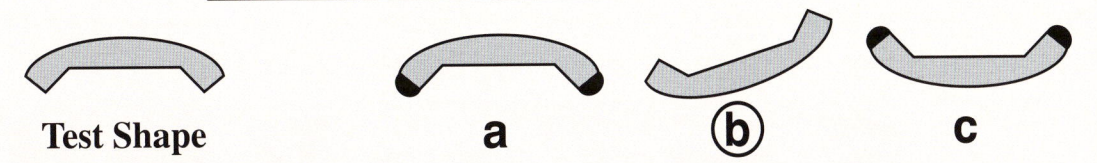

Test Shape   a   ⓑ   c

Answer: **b** - The shape has been rotated but has no additions.

Example 3: Which figure is next in the series?

Answer: **a**

This has an addition of one Triangle with a White Fill at the top of the square and one more Circle with a Black Fill in the middle.

© 2006 Stephen Curran

Exercise 3: 3   Answer the following:

1) Which is the next figure in the series?

Name the shape that should be added.
Answer ____ _____

2) Which pair of figures does not fit in with the others?

Answer ____ The missing overlay shape is a(n) _____.

3) Which pair of figures belongs to this family of figures?

Answer ____
Two linked _____ Shapes of different sizes must be added.

4) Which pair of figures is most like the Test Figures?

Test Figures

Answer ____ Three _____ Shapes with the correct fills must be added.

5) Which pair of figures is the odd one out?

Answer ____ How many smaller shapes should have been added? _____ shape(s)

6) Which pair of figures does not fit in with the other figures?

    a   b   c   d

Answer ____ The added shape should have a _____ fill.

7) Which pair of figures is most like the Test Figures?

Test Figures

Answer ____ How many shapes need to be added? ____ shape(s)

8) Which pair of figures does not fit in with the others?

    a   b   c   d

Answer ____
Why not? _____

9) Which is the next figure in the series?

Answer ____

The correct order of block fills is:
____ ____ ____ ____

10) Which pair of figures belongs to this family of figures?

A→B   B→C   a S→T   b J→K
                       c L→N   d F→G

Answer ____
The three rules are:
i) _____
ii) _____
iii) _____

Score ____

4. Subtraction

In Non-verbal Reasoning, smaller shapes or parts of a shape can be **Subtracted** from the original shape or shapes.

1. Subtracting parts of shapes

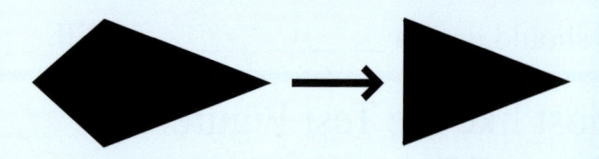

The original Kite with a Block Black Fill has had a Triangular section subtracted from it. The shape that remains is an Isosceles Triangle with a Block Black Fill.

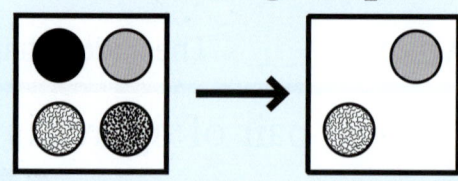

2. Subtracting shapes

The Circles with a Speckled Fill and a Block Black Fill have been subtracted from the original group. This can also be understood as a change in Frequency (see pages 47-49).

Key Non-verbal Reasoning questions apply to subtractions:

Example 1: Which shape is a subtraction of the Test Shape?

Answer: **c** - It has a subtraction or missing piece.

Example 2: Which shape is not a subtraction of the Test Shape?

Answer: **d** - This shape has been rotated but it is the same.

Example 3: Which figure is next in the series?

Answer: **a**

It is a 90° Anticlockwise rotation. The Ribbon Shape with a Block Black Fill is subtracted as it moves to the bottom left of the square.

Exercise 3: 4   Answer the following:

1) Which is the next figure in the series?

Answer ____

A _____ must be subtracted each time in a(n) _____ direction around the shape.

2) Which pair of figures does not fit in with the others?

Answer ____   What two things must be subtracted each time?

i) _____   ii) _____

3) Which figure is next in the series?

What two things must be subtracted?

Answer ____   i) _____   ii) _____

4) Which pair of figures does not fit in with the others?

Why not? _____

Answer ____   _____

5) Which is the next figure in the series?

Answer ____

What is the order of subtraction? (Underline the correct answer.)
Vertical then Horizontal figure **or** Horizontal then Vertical figure.

© 2006 Stephen Curran

6) Which two pairs of shapes are most alike?

a   b   c   d

Answer ____ and ____ Which two things must be subtracted each time?

i) _____ ii) _____

7) Which pair of figures is the odd one out?

a   b   c   d

Answer ____ What must be subtracted each time?

_____

8) Which pair of figures is most like the Test Figures?

Test Figures   a   b   c

Which two things must be subtracted?

Answer ____ i) _____ ii) _____

9) Which figure is next in the series?

a   b
?
c   d

Answer ____

What must be subtracted? _____

10) Which pair of figures is most like the Test Figures?

Test Figures   a   b   c

Answer ____ Which two things must be subtracted?

i) _____

ii) _____

Score

5. Frequency (Counting)

In Non-verbal Reasoning, **Frequency** involves the counting of shapes, smaller shapes within other shapes, or parts of shapes.

1. Counting shapes

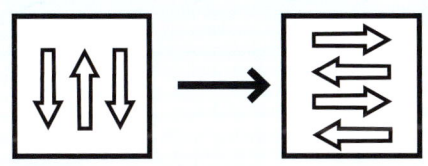

The original figure has three Vertical Arrows. The frequency (number) in the second figure is increased to four Horizontal Arrows. **This change could also be understood as an addition.**

2. Counting parts of shapes

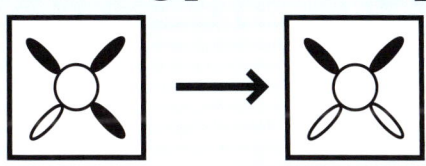

The original figure has three Ellipses with a Black Fill. The frequency (number) in the second figure is decreased to two Ellipses with a Black Fill. **This change could also be understood as a subtraction.**

Key Non-verbal Reasoning questions apply to frequency:

Example 1: Which figure is most similar to the Test Figure?

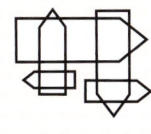

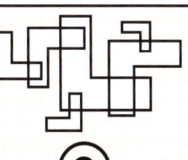

Answer: **c** - It has a frequency of six like the Test Figure.

Example 2: Which figure is most different from the others?

Answer: **e** - It has a frequency of six rather than seven.

Example 3: Which figure is next in the series?

Answer: **b**
The frequency (number) of Squares should be eight. The fill types of the Squares are not relevant. The Equilateral Triangle should point upwards and have Vertical Shading.

© 2006 Stephen Curran

Exercise 3: 5   Answer the following:

1) Which is the next figure in the series?

Answer ____

Write out the number sequence of the six figures.
It begins with **8**, _____

2) Which figure does not fit in with the others?

Answer ____   Why not? _____

3) Which figure belongs to this family of figures?

Answer ____   There should be ____ enclosures inside the shape.

4) Which pair of figures is most like the Test Figures?

Test Figures

Answer ____   How many 'H' letters should there be? ____

5) Which pair of figures is the odd one out?

Answer ____   Why? _____

48   © 2006 Stephen Curran

6) Which figure does not fit in with the other figures?

a   b   c   d

Why not? _____

Answer ____ _____

7) Which figure belongs to this family of figures?

a   b   c

Answer ____ The enclosed shape should have ____ less sides.

8) Which figure does not fit in with the others?

a   b   c   d   e

Answer ____ There should be ____ of each type of line ending.

9) Which is the next figure in the series?

?   a   b   c   d

Answer ____

Write out the number sequence of the six figures.
It begins with **4**, _____

10) Which figure belongs to this family of figures?

a   b   c

Answer ____ Why? _____
_____

Score

© 2006 Stephen Curran

49

Chapter Four
PATTERNS

In Non-verbal Reasoning, shapes can make **Patterns** in two ways:
Repetition • **Cumulation**

1. Repetition

Shapes can be be arranged in a **Repetitive** pattern:

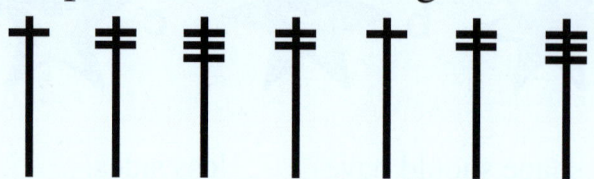

The Telegraph Poles are in a repetitive pattern of one, two, three, two, one, two, three crossbars, etc.

Key Non-verbal Reasoning questions apply to repetition:

Example 1: Which shape is first in the series?

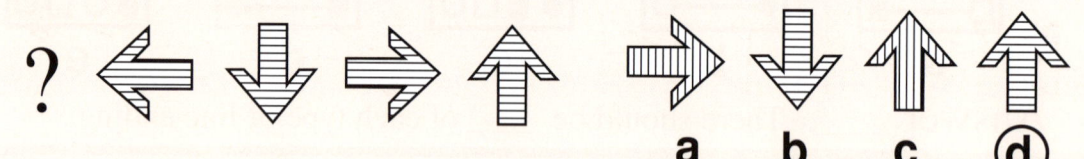

Answer: **d** - It has the correct shading and rotation.

Example 2: Which shape is missing in the series?

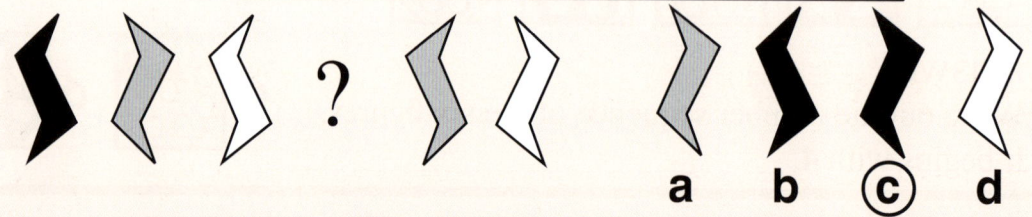

Answer: **c** - It has a Black Fill and is the correct reflection.

Example 3: Which figure is next in the series?

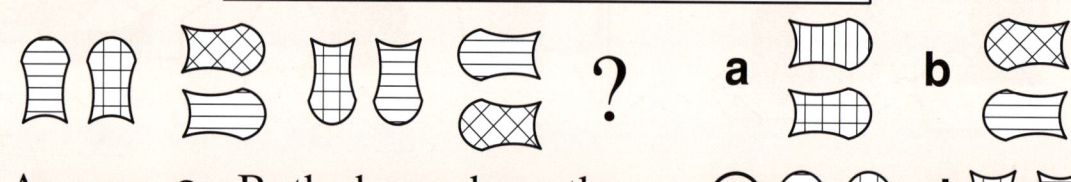

Answer: **c** - Both shapes have the correct fill and rotation.

50 © 2006 Stephen Curran

Exercise 4: 1   Answer the following:

1) Which is the next figure in the series?

Answer ____

Write out the repetitive pattern of the Squares with a Black Fill in numerical terms: _____

2) Which figure is first in the series?

Answer ____   Do the Shaded Fills rotate Clockwise or Anticlockwise? _____

3) Which is the missing figure in the series?

Answer ____   As the shapes are rotated, what kind of movement takes place? _____

4) Which is the next figure in the series?

Answer ____

Write out the order of fills for the Ellipses given in the answer: _____

5) Which figure is first in the series?

Answer ____

Describe the fill of the Triangle in this figure.
_____

© 2006 Stephen Curran

6) Which is the missing figure in the series?

Answer _____ Write out the repetitive pattern of the Asterisks in numerical terms: _____

7) Which figure is next in the series?

Answer _____ Which shape is repeated in every other figure of the series? _____

8) Which figure is next in the series?

Answer _____ Write out the order of fills for the Ellipses: _____

9) Which figure is missing in the series?

Answer _____ Describe the three-fold size progression for the Circle: _____ _____ _____

10) Which is the next figure in the series?

Answer _____
Study the Square Shape.

The Black Fill rotates in a(n) _____ direction.

The Grey Fill rotates in a(n) _____ direction.

52 © 2006 Stephen Curran

2. Cumulation

Shapes can be be arranged in a **Cumulative** pattern:

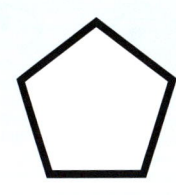

The Pentagon builds side by side in five stages.

Key Non-verbal Reasoning questions apply to cumulation:

Example 1: Which shape is first in the series?

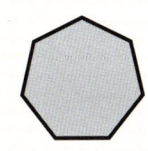

Answer: **b** is a larger shape and has the correct Liquid Fill.

Example 2: Which figure is missing in the series?

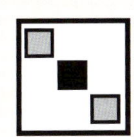

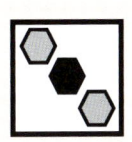

Answer: **d** has Pentagons that lie diagonally from bottom left to top right and has a fill order of Black, Grey, Black.

Example 3: Which figure is next in the series?

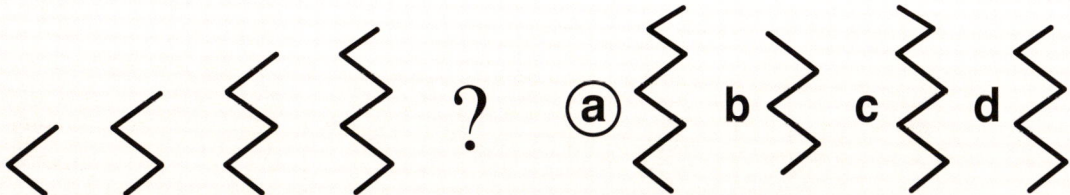

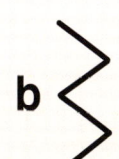

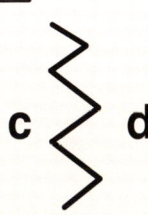

Answer: **a** has six lines so it is the correct Zigzag Line Shape. It is also the correct direction of the Zigzag Line Shape.

© 2006 Stephen Curran

Exercise 4: 2   Answer the following:

1) Which is the next figure in the series?

Answer ____   Name the three shapes used each time:
_____ _____ _____

2) Which figure is first in the series?

Answer ____   Name the two types of line used:
i) _____   ii) _____

3) Which is the missing figure in the series?

Answer ____   Which shape must be subtracted each time? _____

4) Which is the next figure in the series?

Answer ____   Which shape is cumulative? _____

5) Which figure is first in the series?

Answer ____   Each time, which shape must be:
i) added? _____   ii) subtracted? _____

54   © 2006 Stephen Curran

6) Which is the missing figure in the series?

Answer ____   Which shape is added?
_____

7) Which is the next figure in the series?

Answer ____ Name the two cumulative actions:
i) _____
ii) _____

8) Which figure is first in the series?

What must be subtracted?
Answer ____ _____

9) Which is the missing figure in the series?

Answer ____   What shape is subtracted?
_____

10) Which is the next figure in the series?

Answer ____
Name the repetitive pattern of the fills sequence
of the Squares: _____

The cumulative actions are: _____

Score

Chapter Five
LAYERING

Non-verbal Reasoning questions are complicated by the process of **Layering**. Questions can have up to five layers (or changes) that have to be observed to find a solution.

1. Level One

Some shapes only have one layer or change.

The Segment Shape has received only one layer or change. It has been rotated 180°.

Key Non-verbal Reasoning questions apply to layering:

Example 1: Which shape is most similar to the Test Shape?

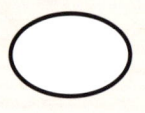

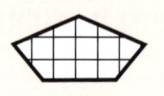

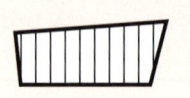

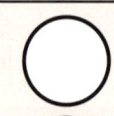

Answer: **d** is circular, as is the Test Shape.

Example 2: Which shape is most unlike the Test Shape?

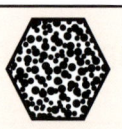

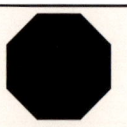

Answer: **c** has a Black Fill; the Test Shape has a Speckled Fill.

Example 3: Which shape is next in the series?

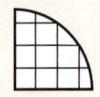

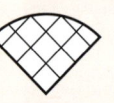

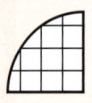

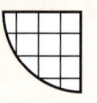

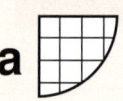

Answer: **b** has been rotated 45° in an Anticlockwise direction.

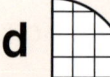

56 © 2006 Stephen Curran

Exercise 5: 1   Answer the following:

1) Which is the next shape in the series?

Answer ____

2) Which shape does not fit in with the others?

Answer ____

3) Which figure belongs to this family of figures?

Answer ____

4) Which figure is most like the Test Figure?

Test Figure

Answer ____

5) Which shape is the odd one out?

Answer ____

© 2006 Stephen Curran

6) Which figure does not fit in with the others?

a   b   c   d   e

Answer ____

7) Which figure is most similar to the Test Figures?

Test Figures

a   b   c   d

Answer ____

8) Which figure is the odd one out?

a   b   c   d   e

Answer ____

9) Which figure is next in the series?

?   a   b   c   d

Answer ____

10) Which figure is most similar to the Test Figures?

Test Figures

a   b   c

Answer ____   Score

© 2006 Stephen Curran

2. Level Two

In Non-verbal Reasoning, questions can have two layers:

Test Shape → **Layer 1** → **Layer 2**

The Pencil Shape has two layers (undergoes two changes):
Layer 1 - It has been reflected or rotated 180°.
Layer 2 - The Block Black Fill becomes a Block Grey Fill.

Example 1: Which shape completes the second pair of shapes?

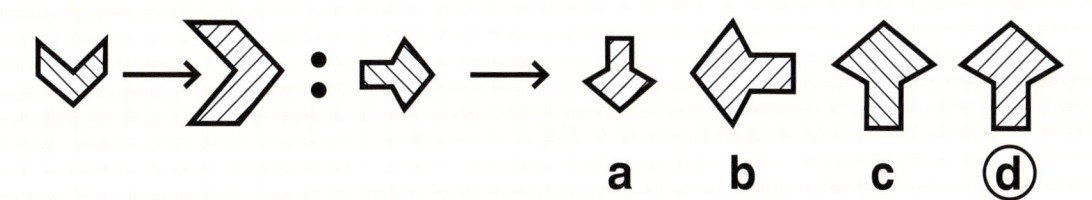

a b c **d**

Answer: **d** - The shape enlarges and rotates 90° Anticlockwise (in the same way as the first pair).

Example 2: Which pair of shapes is the odd one out?

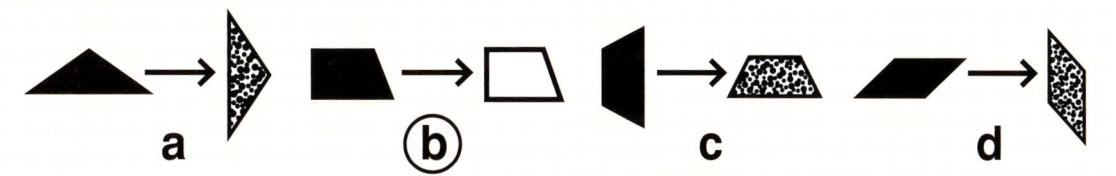

a **b** c d

Answer: **b** does not rotate and has the wrong fill.

Example 3: Which figure is next in the series?

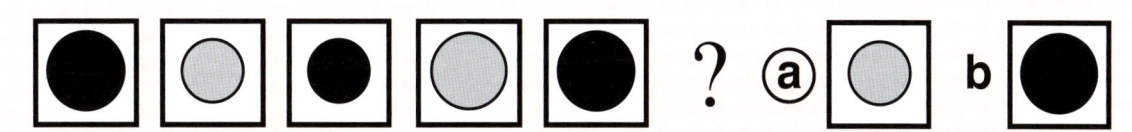

a b c d

Answer: **a** has a Grey Fill (fills alternate) and it has a small Circle. (Pattern is two small Circles, then two large Circles, etc.)

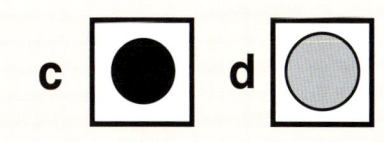

© 2006 Stephen Curran

Exercise 5: 2   Answer the following:

1) Which is the next figure in the series?

Answer ____

2) Which figure is most like the Test Figure?

Test Figure   a   b   c   d

Answer ____

3) Which is the next figure in the series?

Answer ____

4) Which figure is most similar to the Test Figure?

Test Figure   a   b   c   d

Answer ____

5) Which figure is next in the series?

Answer ____

© 2006 Stephen Curran

6) Which two figures are most similar?

a   b   c   d   e

Answer ____ and ____

7) Which figure is most like the Test Figure?

Test Figure   a   b   c   d

Answer ____

8) Which figure is most similar to the Test Figure?

Test Figure   a   b   c   d

Answer ____

9) Which is the next figure in the series?

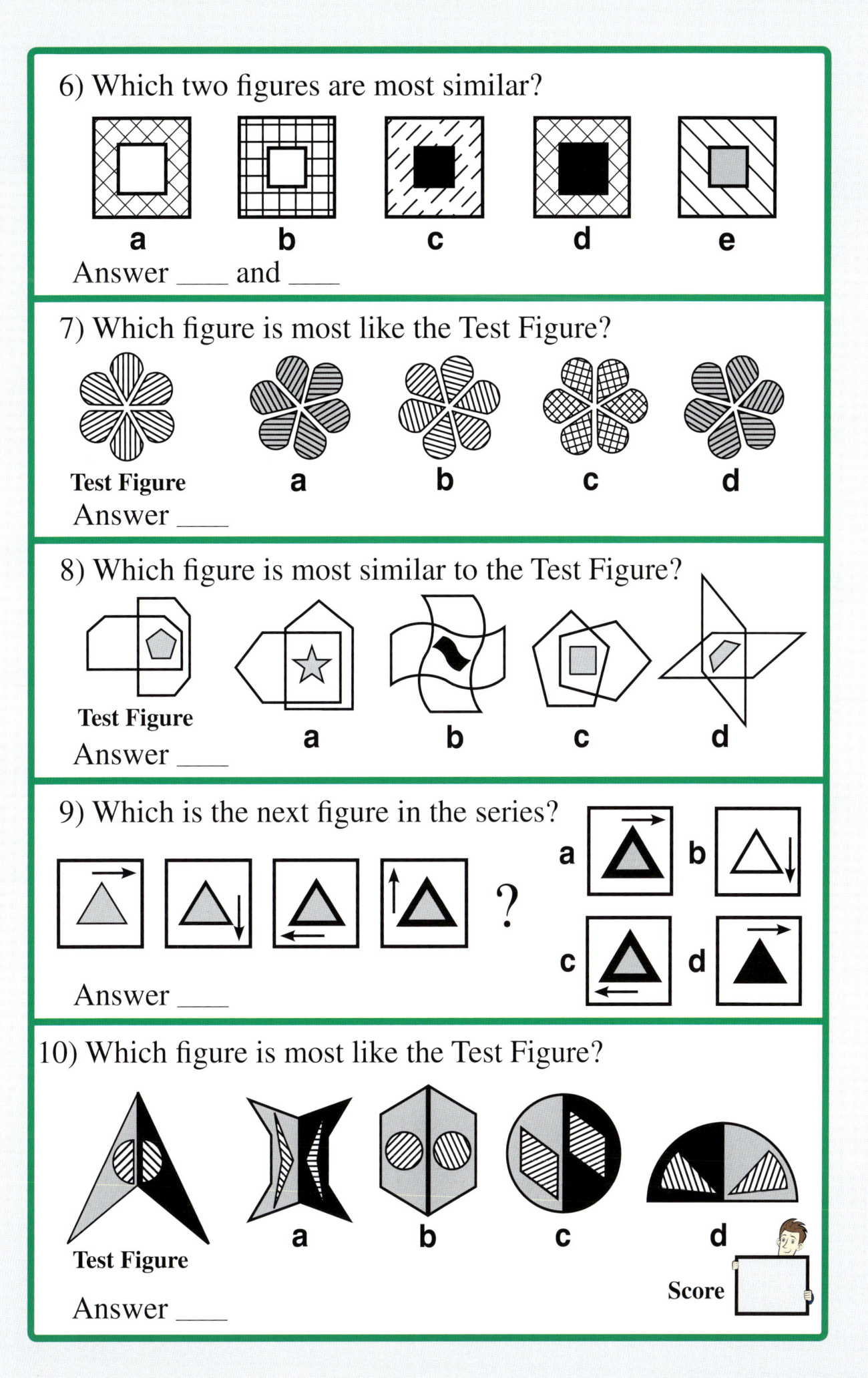

? a b c d

Answer ____

10) Which figure is most like the Test Figure?

Test Figure   a   b   c   d

Answer ____

Score

© 2006 Stephen Curran

3. Level Three

In Non-verbal Reasoning, questions can have three layers:

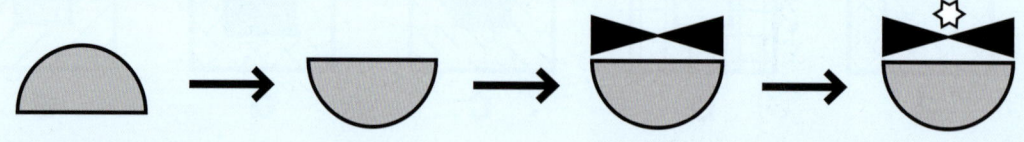

Test Shape → Layer 1 → Layer 2 → Layer 3

The Semi-circle has three layers (undergoes three changes):
Layer 1 - It has been rotated 180° or flipped Vertically.
Layer 2 - A Black Filled Bow Tie Shape is added at the top.
Layer 3 - A White Filled Star is added at the top.

Example 1: Which shape completes the second pair of shapes?

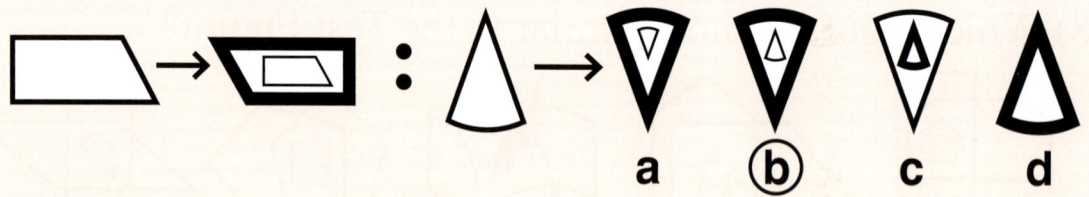

Answer: **b** - The outer shape rotates 180°; the line becomes thicker; a smaller but identical inner shape is enclosed within the outer shape.

Example 2: Which figure is the odd one out?

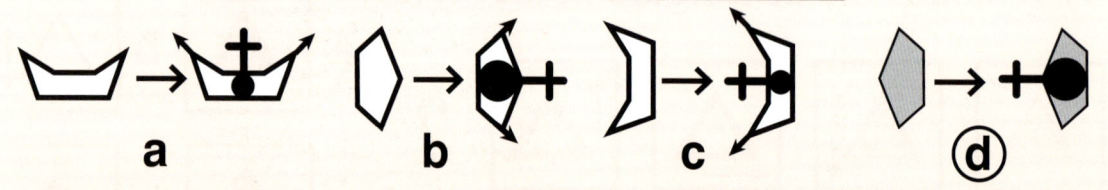

Answer: **d** - The Boat Shape should receive the three additions; **d** has a Circle with a Black Fill and a Black Cross Shape but no Arrow Shapes.

Example 3: Which figure is next in the series?

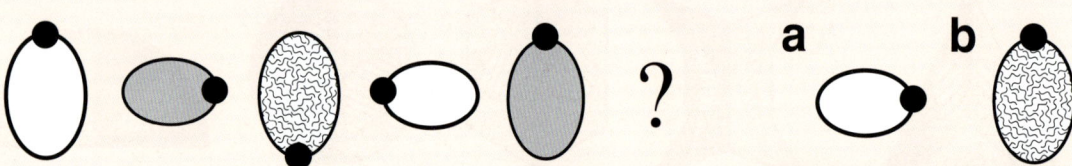

Answer: **c** - It has a Mottled Fill, both shapes rotate 90° Clockwise and the Ellipse reduces in size.

62 © 2006 Stephen Curran

Exercise 5: 3   Answer the following:

1) Which is the next figure in the series?

Answer ____

2) Which figure is most similar to the Test Figure?

Test Figure

Answer ____

3) Which figure is most like the Test Figure?

Test Figure

Answer ____

4) Which figure completes the second pair of figures?

Answer ____

5) Which figure is most similar to the Test Figures?

Test Figures

Answer ____

© 2006 Stephen Curran

6) Which figure is most like the Test Figure?

Test Figure   a   b   c   d

Answer ____

7) Which figure is most similar to the Test Figure?

Test Figure   a   b   c   d

Answer ____

8) Which is the next figure in the series?

Answer ____

9) Which figure is most similar to the Test Figure?

Test Figure   a   b   c   d

Answer ____

10) Which figure is most similar to the Test Figures?

Test Figures   a   b   c   d

Answer ____

Score

© 2006 Stephen Curran

4. Level Four

In Non-verbal Reasoning, questions can have four layers:

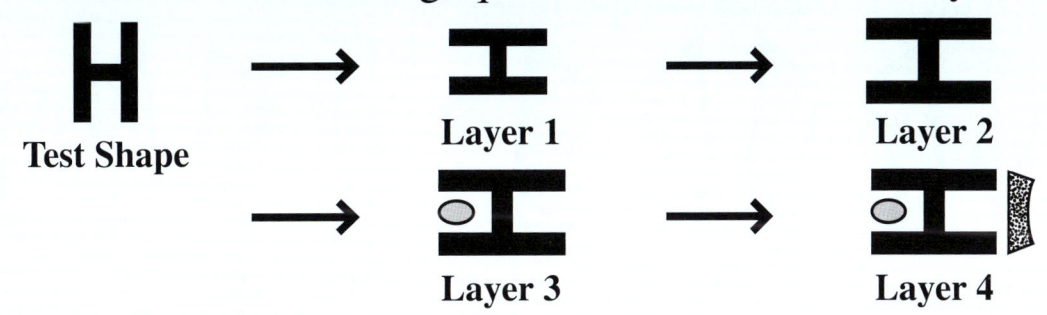

Test Shape H → **Layer 1** → **Layer 2** → **Layer 3** → **Layer 4**

The Letter Shape has four layers (undergoes four changes):
Layer 1 - 'H' Shape rotated 90°.   **Layer 2** - 'H' Shape enlarged.
Layer 3 - Oval with a Grey Fill is added to the 'H' Shape.
Layer 4 - Blade Shape with a Liquid Fill is added to the 'H' Shape.

Example 1: Which figure completes the second pair of figures?

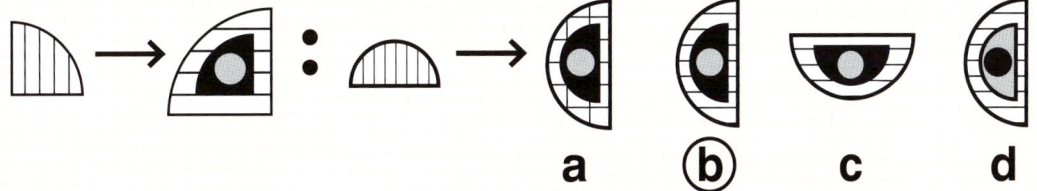

a   b   c   d

Answer: **b** - Shape rotates 90° Anticlockwise; figure enlarges; smaller identical inner shape with Black Fill added; Circle with Grey Fill added.

Example 2: Which pair of shapes is the odd one out?

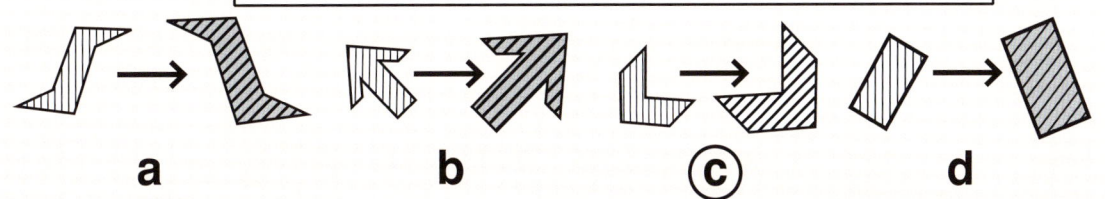

a   b   c   d

Answer: **c** - Chevrons reflect or flip Horizontally; Diagonal Lines rotate 45° Clockwise; reflected shape gets larger but there is no Grey Fill.

Example 3: Which figure is next in the series?

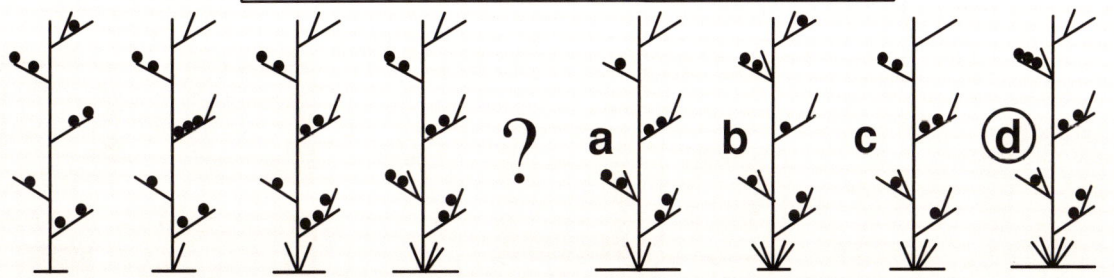

?   a   b   c   d

Answer: **d** - One Circle transposes (moves) from Line to Line; one Line is added; the base enlarges; one more Line is added at the base.

© 2006 Stephen Curran

Exercise 5: 4 Answer the following:

1) Which is the next shape in the series?

Answer ____   a   b   c   d

2) Which figure is most similar to the Test Figure?

Test Figure

Answer ____   a   b   c   d   e

3) Which is the next figure in the series?

Answer ____

4) Which figure completes the second pair of figures?

a   b   c   d   e

Answer ____

5) Which is the next figure in the series?

Answer ____

66   © 2006 Stephen Curran

6) Which figure is most like the Test Figure?

Test Figure

a b c d e f

Answer ____

7) Which two figures are most similar?

a b c d e

Answer ____ and ____

8) Which figure is most like the Test Figure?

Test Figure

a b c d e

Answer ____

9) Which figure is next in the series?

a b c d

Answer ____

10) Which figure is most similar to the Test Figure?

Test Figure

a b c d e

Answer ____

Score

5. Level Five

In Non-verbal Reasoning, questions can have five layers:

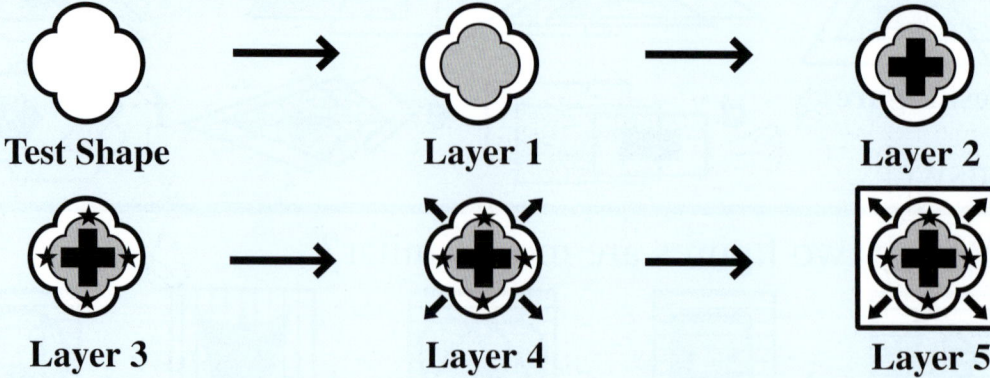

Test Shape → **Layer 1** → **Layer 2**

Layer 3 → **Layer 4** → **Layer 5**

The Flower Shape has five layers (undergoes five changes):
Layer 1 - Grey Filled Flower Shape is enclosed. **Layer 2** - Black Filled Cross is superimposed. **Layer 3** - Four Stars are superimposed.
Layer 4 - Four Arrows are added. **Layer 5** - Square encloses the shapes.

Example 1: Which figure completes the second pair of figures?

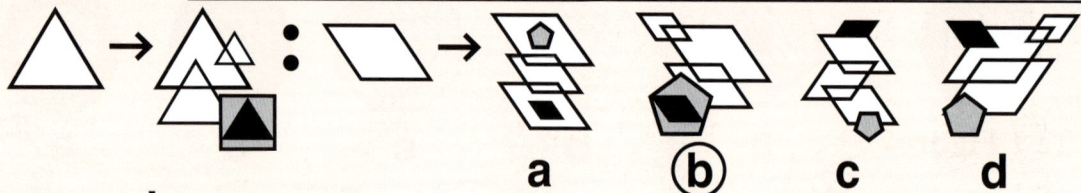

Answer: **b** - Two Rhombuses are added; the Rhombuses are reduced in size; all the Rhombuses are linked; the Pentagon is overlayed; the Black Filled Rhombus is enclosed.

Example 2: Which pair of figures is the odd one out?

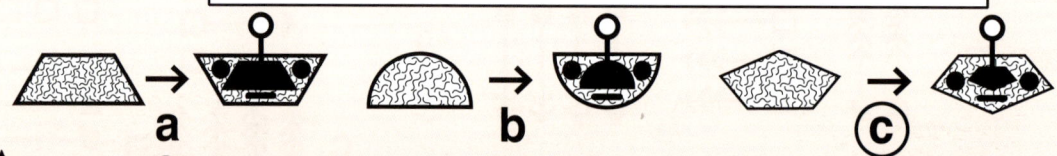

Answer: **c** - The outer Pentagon rotates 180°; a Line Ending with a Circle is added; two Circles with Black Fills are added; a Thick Black Line is added but the Enclosed Pentagon with a Black Fill has not been rotated.

Example 3: Which figure is next in the series?

Answer: **a** - One of every shape is subtracted each time; all the shapes are flipped (reflected) Horizontally; the fills alternate between Black and White in the Squares; the Speaker Shapes rotate 90° Clockwise; one Arrow receives a Black Fill diagonally each time.

Exercise 5: 5   Answer the following:

1) Which is the next figure in the series?

Answer ____

2) Which figure is most similar to the Test Figure?

Answer ____

3) Which figure is most similar to the Test Figures?

Answer ____

4) Which figure is most like the Test Figure?

Answer ____

5) Which figure is most similar to the Test Figure?

Answer ____

© 2006 Stephen Curran

6) Which figure is most like the Test Figures?

Test Figures

Answer ____   a   b   c   d   e

7) Which figure is most similar to the Test Figures?

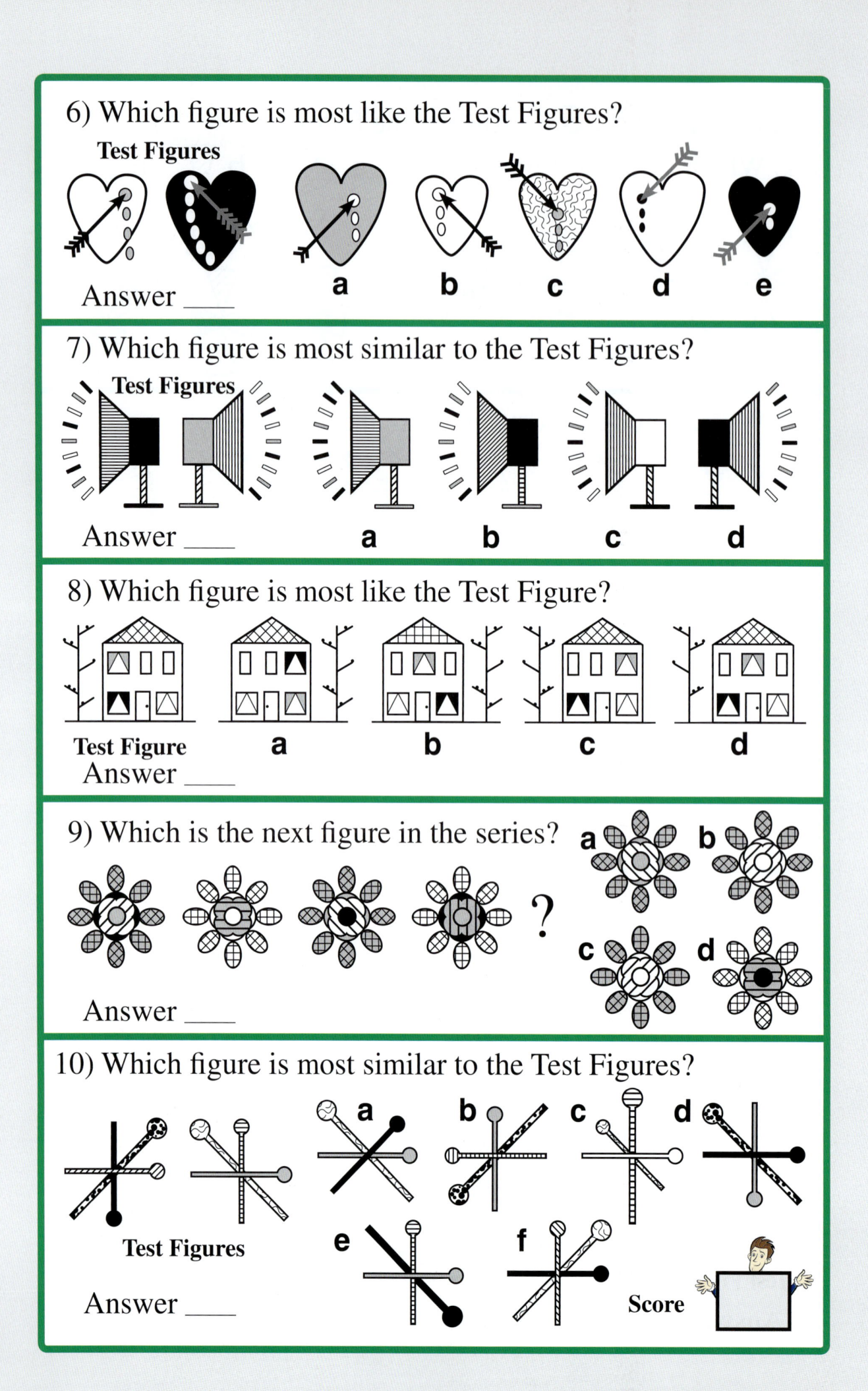

Test Figures

Answer ____   a   b   c   d

8) Which figure is most like the Test Figure?

Test Figure
Answer ____   a   b   c   d

9) Which is the next figure in the series?

a   b

c   d

Answer ____

10) Which figure is most similar to the Test Figures?

a   b   c   d

Test Figures

e   f

Answer ____   Score

70   © 2006 Stephen Curran

Answers

Chapter One
Elements

Exercise 1: 1
1) Quadrant
2) Arrowhead
3) Segment
4) Regular Octagon
5) Regular Hexagon
6) Trapezium
7) Ellipse
8) Parallelogram
9) Regular Nonagon
10) Scalene Triangle

Exercise 1: 2
1) Bone
2) Sea Horse
3) Speaker
4) Churn
5) Blade
6) Helmet
7) Boat
8) Flower
9) Wizard's Hat
10) Chevron

Exercise 1: 3
1) **b** - Regular Decagon
2) **c** - House/Irregular Pentagon
3) **b** - Ribbon or Flag
4) **e** - Straight Arrow
5) **b** - Equilateral Triangle
6) **d** - Helmet
7) **c** - Isosceles Triangle
8) **d** - Irregular Heptagon
9) **a** - Six-pointed Star
10) **c** - General Quadrilateral

Exercise 1: 4
1) Block/Grey
2) Cross-hatched/Lattice
3) Shaded/Vertical/Solid
4) Liquid/Speckled
5) Cross-hatched/Squares
6) Shaded/Left Slant/Dashed
7) Dotted/Close
8) Liquid/Mottled
9) Shaded/Horizontal/Dashed
10) Shaded/Right Slant/Solid

Exercise 1: 5
1) **a** - Block/Grey
2) **d** - Cross-hatched/Squares
3) **b** - Shaded/Horizontal/Solid
4) **d** - Shaded/Vertical/Solid
5) **b** - Liquid/Mottled
6) **b/e** - Liquid/Speckled
7) **c** - Shaded/Left Slant/Dashed
8) **b** - Block/Black
9) **b** - Cross-hatched/Lattice
10) **e** - Liquid/Speckled

Exercise 1: 6a
1) Dotted/Straight/Thin; Cross.
2) Solid/Straight/Thick; Symbol.
3) Dashed/Straight/Thin; Pitchfork.
4) Dashed/Straight/Thin; Letter.
5) Solid/Straight/Thin; Zigzag.

Exercise 1: 6b
6) Dashed/Curved/Thin; Wave.
7) Solid/CurvedThick; Fish.
8) Solid/Curved/Thin; Pulleys.
9) Dotted/Curved/Thin; Curved Arrow.
10) Solid/Curved/Thick; Basin.

Exercise 1: 7
1) **b** - Telegraph Poles
2) **c** - Straight Arrows
3) **b** - Grille
4) **c** - Symbol
5) **d** - Curved Arrow
6) **d** - Solid/Straight/Thick
7) **b** - Dashed/Curved/Thin
8) **e** - Dotted/Straight/Thin
9) **b** - Symbols
10) **b** - Dotted/Straight/Thin

Exercise 1: 8
1) **a** - The order of fills is Grey, Black, White.
2) **b** - It is rotated at 45° or Diagonally, whereas the others are positioned either Vertically or Horizontally.

11+ Non-verbal Reasoning Year 5-7 Workbook 1

Answers

3) **c** - The fills alternate Grey/Dotted/Grey and the sides lessen by two each time.
4) **d** - It only has five sides whereas all the other shapes have six sides.
5) **d** - The shape rotates 180° each time and the shading rotates 45° Clockwise each time.
6) **c** and **e** - The shapes have Slanted Shading.
7) **c** - It has a Black Fill whereas the others have either White or Grey Fills.
8) **b** - It has an odd number of sides like the Test Shape.
9) **a** - The Star Shape must be smaller with a Liquid (Mottled) Fill.
10) **a** - It is a standard, one-sided Circular Shape like the Test Shape.

Chapter Two
Movements
Exercise 2: 1
1) **b** - Shaded/Right Slanted Solid
2) **d** - Chevrons
3) **a** - Liquid/Speckled and Mottled
4) **d** - It is a Helmet and not a Shield.
5) **c** - M is the next letter that has a Reflective Line of Symmetry.
6) **a** and **d** - Both pairs of shapes reflect.
7) **e** - i) The shapes reflect.
ii) Ribbons or Flags
8) **b** - Blade
9) **a** - Sector
10) **b** - Bean

Exercise 2: 2
1) **b** - 45°; Anticlockwise.
2) **b** - 180°
3) **a** - 90° Clockwise
4) **c** - 90° and 180°
5) **d** - Clockwise
6) **e** - The shading goes in the same direction.
7) **c** - The Arrow goes in a Clockwise direction.
8) **c** - 180°
9) **b** - 45°; 90°; Anticlockwise.
10) **a** - The letter F only rotates once (360°).

Exercise 2: 3
1) **a** - Vertical inversion or flip.
2) **b** - It is an inversion; the other shapes are rotations.
3) **d** - Horizontal and Vertical inversion (rotated 180°).
4) **a** - It can only be seen as a Horizontal inversion, whereas the others are all 180° rotations.
5) **c** - It rotates 90°, has a Grey Fill and is inverted Horizontally.
6) **a** and **c** - They match as rotations, whereas the others are inversions.
7) **c** - All the letters have been rotated 180° (double flipped), but the letter F is a Vertical inversion.
8) **d** - It is an inversion of the Test Shape and will not rotate.
9) **d** - The pattern is a Vertical inversion or flip, then reflection, etc; The fill order is Shading, Shading, Liquid (Mottled) Fill.
10) **c** - It is the only Horizontally inverted or flipped figure.

Exercise 2: 4
1) **c** - Merger
2) **e** - Overlay
3) **a** - Linkage
4) **b** - Enclosure
5) **d** - Overlay
6) **c** - Merger/Linkage
7) **d** - Enclosure
8) **c** - Merger
9) **b** - Overlay
10) **b** - Overlay/Linkage/ Enclosure

11+ Non-verbal Reasoning Year 5-7 Workbook 1

Answers

Exercise 2: 5
1) **d** - Grey Fill/Horizontal; White Fill/Vertical; Black Fill/Horizontal.
2) **a** - Flower/Horizontal; Straight Arrow/Vertical; Circle/Vertical.
3) **d** - Circle/Vertical; Pentagon/Horizontal.
4) **c** - Horizontal and Vertical
5) **b** - Octagon/Vertical; Kite/Horizontal.
6) **b** - Curved Arrow/Horizontal; F Shape/Vertical and Horizontal.
7) **d** - Horizontal
8) **a** - Black Shape/Horizontal; Grey Shape/Vertical.
9) **d** - Vertical
10) **b** - Vertical and Horizontal

Chapter Three
Manipulations
Exercise 3: 1
1) **b** - Enlargement
2) **c** - Reduction
3) **d** - Arrow/Reduces Heart/Enlarges
4) **c** - Reduction
5) **b** - Reduction
6) **d** - Enlargement
7) **a** - Reduction
8) **d** - Reduction
9) **c** - Enlargement
10) **a** - Reduction

Exercise 3: 2
1) **d** - Squashed
2) **c** - Stretched
3) **c** - House Shape Stretched; Cross Shape Squashed.
4) **b** - Hexagon
5) **a** - Square
6) **b** and **e** - Stretched
7) **d** - Squashed
8) **b** - Squashed
9) **d** - Stretched
10) **c** - Squashed/Left Stretched/Right

Exercise 3: 3
1) **a** - Isosceles Trapezium
2) **d** - Parallelogram
3) **c** - Speaker
4) **b** - Flower
5) **c** - Two shapes
6) **d** - Black Fill
7) **c** - One shape
8) **a** - Three Ellipses have been added instead of two.
9) **b** - White/Grey/Black/White
10) **b** - i) Rotates 90°
    ii) Next letter in the alphabet.
    iii) Square has a Grey Fill.

Exercise 3: 4
1) **a** - Line/Anticlockwise
2) **c** - i) An enclosed shape.
    ii) A Horizontal Shaded Fill.
3) **a** - i) An Arrowhead.
    ii) The fill gets lighter.
4) **d** - The wrong Diagonal Line has been subtracted on the Square.
5) **a** - Vertical then Horizontal.
6) **a** and **c** - i) A quarter of the shape is subtracted.
    ii) The fill is subtracted and replaced by a White Fill.
7) **c** - Two shapes with Grey Fills must be subtracted.
8) **c** - i) The Shaded Fill
    ii) The outer shape with a Dashed Line
9) **b** - Circle with a White Fill
10) **a** - i) One merged shape
    ii) The smallest enclosed shape

Exercise 3: 5
1) **c** - 8, 1, 6, 3, 4, 5
2) **a** - A Five-pointed Star with a White Fill has replaced a Cross with a White Fill. It now has six Five-pointed Stars rather than five.
3) **b** - Four enclosures
4) **c** - Five H Letters
5) **b** - There must be two of each type of Cross.

Answers

11+ Non-verbal Reasoning Year 5-7 Workbook 1

6) **b** - One of the Shields with a Black Fill should have a Grey Fill.
7) **c** - Two less sides.
8) **e** - Four of each.
9) **d** - 4, 3, 6, 5, 8, 7
10) **c** - The three shapes must have a consecutive number of sides, e.g. 5, 6, 7 sides, etc.

Chapter Four
Patterns
Exercise 4: 1
1) **a** - 1, 2, 3, 2, 1, etc.
2) **a** - Anticlockwise
3) **d** - Reflection
4) **d** - White/Grey Mottled/White
5) **c** - Shaded Fill/Right Slanted Solid Line
6) **c** - 6, 5, 3, 5, 6
7) **b** - Five-pointed Star
8) **a** - White/Black/Grey/White/Black, etc.
9) **b** - Each shape changes size in the order: small, medium, large, small, etc.
10) **a** - Black Fill rotates Clockwise; Grey Fill rotates Anticlockwise.

Exercise 4: 2
1) **b** - Heart, Churn, Bulb
2) **a** - Dashed, Straight and Thin; Solid, Straight and Thick.

3) **b** - Parallelogram
4) **c** - Flower Shape
5) **d** - Add a Solid Line; subtract Phone Shape.
6) **c** - A Circle with a Block Black Fill.
7) **d** - i) Solid Line gets thinner.
ii) The Black Fill is replaced by a White Fill in the Squares.
8) **c** - One Arrowhead.
9) **a** - A Semi-circle with a Speckled Fill.
10) **c** - Squares fill sequence: Grey/Black/White/Grey; cumulative action: Triangles and Circles enlarge.

Chapter Five
Layering
Exercise 5: 1
1) **c**
2) **b**
3) **c**
4) **d**
5) **c**
6) **e**
7) **c**
8) **d**
9) **d**
10) **b**

Exercise 5: 2
1) **c**
2) **b**
3) **b**
4) **c**
5) **a**

6) **a** and **d**
7) **b**
8) **c**
9) **a**
10) **d**

Exercise 5: 3
1) **d**
2) **d**
3) **c**
4) **c**
5) **b**
6) **a**
7) **b**
8) **c**
9) **d**
10) **b**

Exercise 5: 4
1) **a**
2) **d**
3) **a**
4) **c**
5) **c**
6) **e**
7) **c** and **e**
8) **c**
9) **a**
10) **d**

Exercise 5: 5
1) **d**
2) **d**
3) **b**
4) **d**
5) **e**
6) **b**
7) **d**
8) **c**
9) **b**
10) **b**

PROGRESS CHARTS

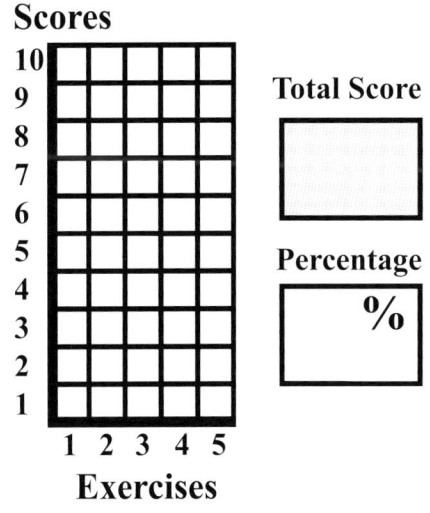

1. ELEMENTS

Scores

Exercises: 1 2 3 4 5 6 7 8

Total Score

Percentage %

2. MOVEMENTS

Scores

Exercises: 1 2 3 4 5

Total Score

Percentage %

3. MANIPULATIONS

Scores

Exercises: 1 2 3 4 5

Total Score

Percentage %

4. PATTERNS

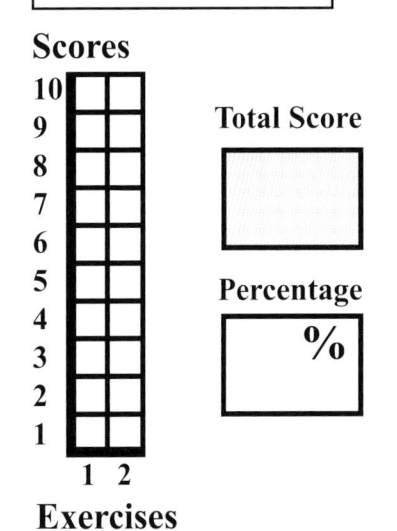

Scores

Exercises: 1 2

Total Score

Percentage %

5. LAYERING

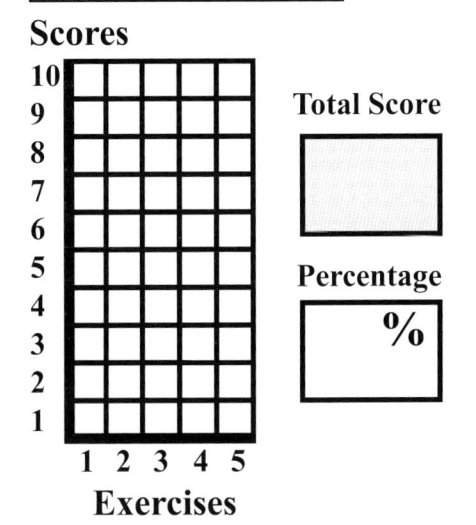

Scores

Exercises: 1 2 3 4 5

Total Score

Percentage %

Shade in your score for each exercise on the graphs. Add up for your total score.

For the average add up % and divide by 5

Overall Percentage

%

© 2006 Stephen Curran

75

CERTIFICATE OF ACHIEVEMENT

This certifies

_____

has successfully completed

11+ Non-verbal Reasoning
Year 5–7
WORKBOOK 1

Overall percentage score achieved [ ] %

Comment _____

_____

Signed _____
(teacher/parent/guardian)

Date _____